PILLARS FOR LIFE: A GUIDE TO SPIRITUAL ETHICS AND PRACTICE

for Light Workers, Healers, Psychics, Mediums, Shamans, Energy Workers, and All Souls Called to Shine Their Light

Catherine Crestani

Copyright © 2025 Catherine Crestani

Pillars for Life: A Guide to Spiritual Ethics and Practice

Paperback ISBN: 978-1-7641507-0-5
Ebook ISBN: 978-1-7641507-3-6

The moral rights of the author have been asserted.

All rights reserved. No part of this publication may be reproduced, stored in a retrieval system, or transmitted in any form or by any means—electronic, mechanical, photocopying, recording, or otherwise—without the prior written permission of the copyright holder, except for brief quotations used in reviews or scholarly works.

This book is a work of nonfiction intended for educational and inspirational purposes. The author and publisher have made every effort to ensure the accuracy of the information herein but make no guarantees and disclaim liability for any errors or omissions. The content is not intended as a substitute for professional advice or guidance.

Cover design by Peter Jones
Printed in Australia
First Edition

For permission requests, please contact:
hello@willowhealing.org

*To Carli Sherriff for reawakening my sleeping soul
and Chiron Yeng for pushing me to be infinite.*

CONTENTS

Title Page
Copyright
Dedication
Foreword
Chapter 1 The World Has Been Waiting — 1
Chapter 2 Spiritual Ethics Framework — 6
Chapter 3 Pillar 1: Divine Will — 12
Chapter 4 Pillar 2: Authenticity — 23
Chapter 5 Pillar 3: Presence — 32
Chapter 6 Pillar 4: Willingness to Change — 42
Chapter 7 Pillar 5: Spiritual Responsibility — 52
Chapter 8 Pillar 6: Equality — 66
Chapter 9 Pillar 7: Accountability — 74
Chapter 10 Groundwork: Be Connected to Earth — 84
Chapter 11 Foundation: Knowing Yourself and Others — 92
Chapter 12 Keystone: Remember to be Human — 101
Chapter 13 Bringing it All Together — 108
References — 112
Acknowledgement — 115
About The Author — 117

FOREWORD

Every once in a while, a book comes along that feels less like something new and more like something we've been waiting for, something our hearts already knew, but hadn't yet found the words for. *Pillars for Life – A Guide to Spiritual Ethics and Practice* by Catherine Crestani is exactly that kind of book.

In a world where so much feels uncertain, overwhelming, or disconnected, this book offers a grounded, soulful way forward. It's not about escaping the world or reaching for something out of touch. It's about coming home to yourself, your truth, your values, your spiritual center, and learning how to live from that place with clarity, kindness, and courage.

Catherine has laid out a framework that's both deep and refreshingly accessible. The seven spiritual pillars she shares: Divine Will, Authenticity, Presence, Willingness to Change, Spiritual Responsibility, Equality, and Accountability, aren't just lofty concepts. They're practical, lived principles that invite you to show up more fully in your life, your relationships, and your purpose.

What makes this book special is how human it is. Catherine doesn't talk *at* you; she walks *with* you. She reminds us that spiritual growth isn't about being perfect, it's about being real. The chapters on grounding, self-awareness, and remembering our shared humanity are beautiful reminders that spirituality starts right where you are, with your feet on the ground and your heart open.

Whether you're deep into your spiritual practice or just beginning to explore what living a more ethical, soul-centered life might look like, *Pillars for Life* will meet you where you are. It's the kind of book you'll want to return to again and again, not because you missed something, but because each time, you'll be a little more ready to receive it.

So, take a breath. Turn the page. Let this book be your companion on the journey back to what really matters.

Jane Barlow Christensen
(kindred soul)

CHAPTER 1 THE WORLD HAS BEEN WAITING

The spiritual movement and community have evolved rapidly over the past decade. Terms such as "Reiki," "psychics," and "crystals" are no longer considered as woo as they previously were, and you will find science is catching up to the metaphysical practices. The magic of the heart, the healing process involved in grounding, and even the energy attached to our DNA, which allows energy healing, are all being proven through science and studies.

However, the integrity of the shared information and some practices has created a division in the community. The division is between practitioners and those seeking further guidance on their spiritual journey. I have heard many a story of clients having information shared that is not for the highest and greatest good or that is sometimes not even for them. Other reports have included breaches of confidentiality or an unhealthy dependence on the practitioner, which is not empowering the soul on their journey. I, too, have personally experienced my energy being taken rather than restored and being given information that did not resonate as true for me. This left me feeling violated, and I had to work to restore my energy. I chose to follow my own intuition rather than the misaligned channel and information shared. When my energy is imbalanced, it makes it difficult to allow information and energy to flow, which, in turn, hinders me from serving others.

While I have learned to discern what resonates and put in place my own protection, not all souls have this wisdom and can be left feeling different and not in a good way after a session.

It is through these experiences that my mentor, Carli Sheriff, channeled information to share with me and, in turn, the world on professional conduct for light workers, psychics, healers, mediums, guides, shamans, and any spiritual practice. Further intuitive insights have been gifted to me through discussions with other practitioners and serving clients, and as a result, the knowledge has continued to evolve. Carli and my interactions with other practitioners, who we engaged personally or through observations, highlighted the need to bring an idea of guidelines and a framework to conduct ourselves into the spotlight. For example, tarot readers who do not put parameters on the information shared, mediums who channel through information that is not pertinent to the client or soul working with them, seers who predict a timeline that has not yet occurred and, in turn, bring it into fruition, or body workers who leave their energy imparted on the soul they are working with. There has not yet been evidence of these scenarios being highlighted, nor are there any guidelines to refer one back to. As a result, the Spiritual Ethics Framework was shared in order to re-establish a higher level of spiritual ethics for which we can hold ourselves accountable. As the planet and Mother Earth continue to shift their vibrations and/or frequency, these guidelines are important to help us grow, as well as serve any souls who choose to engage our services.

I personally have had experience with the need for such guidelines early in my spiritual journey. After engaging in the services of practitioners to complete a crystal realignment and massage, I was left feeling that my energy had been taken. This led me to feel violated and disappointed, particularly as I was not aware of how to protect my energy at the time and stop this from occurring. It was a valuable lesson in that it caused me to dive deeper into my own spiritual hygiene and how to trust my intuition when it came to engaging other practitioners to work with my energy. Further observations highlighted how telling someone information that they were not ready for, or was not for them, could lead to a set of unprecedented events that impacted negatively on the soul receiving the information and send them into a state of depression. To me, this emphasized and strengthened my resolve to tune further into the wisdom and guidance from the Universe when interacting with any soul I came in contact with, as well as to discern when to share information from intuitive downloads and when to not.

Spirit/Universe/God/Divine/All That Is/Source or whichever term resonates with you has urged me to share this information. The term Universe will be used to encompass this infinite source of wisdom and knowledge throughout this book. The urgency of needing to write this was highlighted as I was told to share the guidelines due to recurring nudges, as the Universe knows it is time for us to open up discussions and have a guidebook, if you will, to support us as we explore the realm of our chosen practice. As I continued to speak with other souls in the spiritual community, there was an overall consensus that the concept of spiritual ethics and guidelines was not only needed but should be an integral part of anyone's practice when serving souls at any level.

Our society has an emphasis on ethics. From ethical boards in professions to human rights, however, there has been a lack of spiritual community. There is no board to complain to and no association with whom to lodge a complaint. I personally have experienced being subject to practices that are not in alignment with the highest and greatest good for myself and the practitioner; however, there is never anything to refer to as to why this felt out of alignment or was against an unspoken ethical code of practice. When serving other souls, whether giving or receiving, we need to hold ourselves accountable and with the highest integrity. It is important for us to be responsible for our conduct and understand that we are impacting another soul's life. When not truly aligned, this can have grave impacts. One such example is a past employee who learned she was pregnant during a group medium reading. She had been trying to conceive and was elated by this news. However, within the week of finding out, she lost the pregnancy and was devastated. Had she not been told the news, she would have assumed that it was another period. This then led to her entering into a state of post-traumatic stress disorder and depression, which took her many months to be able to share and speak about. The information we share and the actions and energy used with another soul can lead to karmic implications should it not be used with the intention of the highest integrity for all souls involved.

All information that is shared in this text is for the highest and greatest good to expand your practice. These tools are to be used with your discernment and to be expanded based on your experiences. I cannot pretend to know how you practice or any challenges that may arise. However, if you are aligned with these guidelines, the answer will intuitively arrive for you on how to move through any situation. Often, we, too, need to learn to trust the Universe and the flow of events that occur. When our practice is no longer in alignment, this is a reflection of lessons we need to search for within.

If you are a soul looking for a way to discern if a practitioner is for you, then this book can give you insight into the qualities you may wish to seek when looking for someone to guide you on your soul journey. The main aspect is to find a practitioner who is open to allowing you to ask questions and taking the time to give meaningful responses rather than deflecting or not being accountable for their own limitations.

The book has been organized to walk you through the framework of spiritual ethics, and in turn, the guidelines have been organized into separate chapters with reference to practices, examples, and energy attunement practices, including chakras, guides, crystals, and more. The first guidelines shared are the pillars, as these were the initial part of the framework channeled to me and hold the most weight in our practices. Additionally, the groundwork, foundation, and keystone are addressed and tied into the pillars as they all entwine with each aspect being shared, encapsulating our body, mind, and soul. The idea and nature are to provide you with a visual representation of how these different aspects interweave with each other to form a solid structure that can be utilized in whichever modality your soul feels pulled to.

My intention for this guideline to spiritual ethics is for any soul who reads these words to understand and feel the need for these guidelines in the world. To use their own discernment and see how these guidelines can be used to elevate your frequency, whether giving or receiving, to re-establish the integrity that has been absent from the spiritual community.

May we tap into our highest timelines and empower all souls we are aligned to encounter.

May you use your intuition and be your beautiful, authentic soul as we enjoy the shift into a world of connection and community, of love and light, where triggers and patterns are shifted and healed so that we can raise the vibration and/or frequency of Earth together.

Much love and gratitude,
Catherine

CHAPTER 2 SPIRITUAL ETHICS FRAMEWORK

We, as humans, often overlook the significant impact our words, actions, and energy can have in this world. Like the "Butterfly Effect," misspeaking what has been channeled, tuning the wrong energy that is not aligned, or not keeping our energy protected can have an ongoing ripple effect that we do not always understand until it is too late. The Universe is forgiving, and we can hold ourselves accountable for these misalignments and prevent further impact.

The Spiritual Ethics Framework is a guideline that the Universe has shared, and it is always your choice if you want to incorporate it into your practice. However, the framework is necessary to hold us in a higher vibration to allow ourselves and the souls we connect with to continue to grow.

The Spiritual Ethics Framework includes seven key pillars: Divine Will, Authenticity, Presence, Willingness to Change, Spiritual Responsibility, Equality and Accountability. It includes a foundation—Knowing Yourself and Others—and an overarching keystone—Remember to Be Human. There is also groundwork —Be Connected to Nature— that is important to take into consideration and use to build the existing framework. It is essentially the Earth beneath the foundation you lay or where we stand. If the Earth is unstable, the foundations will not hold. This is often overlooked even when building a home. Putting in the piers is not enough, and further investigation of what the ground is like underneath needs to be considered. This reflects the importance of ensuring the connection to the ground beneath us is complete and being connected to the Earth in which we live before doing any work that influences ourselves and the souls we are aligned to engage with.

The pillars, groundwork, foundation, and keystone are linked energetically to our first seven major chakras in our body and an additional three chakras outside our body. The major chakras and locations are as follows:

- The root/base chakra (near your perineum)
- The sacral chakra (under your belly button)
- The solar plexus chakra (above your belly button)
- The heart chakra (at your heart, both front and back)
- The throat chakra (at your throat, both front and back)
- The third eye chakra (the space between your eyes)
- The crown chakra (at the top of your head)

The additional chakras outside our body include the Earth chakra, the soul star chakra, and the divine chakra. These, in turn, can be linked to levels in our biofield/aura as well as planes of existence.

The planes of existence include:

- The physical plane (e.g., where our body is)
- The astral plane (e.g., where our dreams and meditation occur)
- The spiritual plane (e.g., where we can connect with our higher self/holy spirit/ soul essence and guides)
- The Angelic/Buddhic plane (e.g., where we connect with enlightened energy beings such as Buddha, Archangels, and so forth)

The groundwork, foundation, and overarching keystone are outside our bodies to commemorate the link between human and outside spiritual influences, including Mother Earth, our higher selves or oversoul, and the memories from our souls. These links tie us into the Universe and infinite wisdom beyond our human body.

The Spiritual Ethics framework has been designed to tie into all levels of the mind, body, and spirit to link in with our existence on the physical plane and transverse the planes we often utilize when completing work. The sixth and seventh planes of existence are not addressed, as the sixth plane contains the Universal Laws, and the seventh plane is God/Universe. These, in the Universe's infinite wisdom, have been excluded from Spiritual Ethics as they oversee and govern all that comes after. The Universal Laws are at their own separate level that cannot be influenced, chosen, or changed. They are unchangeable and are there to protect all souls throughout the Universe and govern over all spirits. Likewise, the God/Universe plane is infinite and can never be influenced.

I have created the following table to show the link between auric layers, planes of existence, chakras, and spiritual ethics.

Auric Layer	Plane	Chakra	Pillar of Spiritual Ethics
Divine Gateway	Angelic/ Buddhic Plane	Divine	Keystone
Real Self		Soul Star	Foundation
Earth Star		Earth Chakra	Ground work
Causal Body/ Ketheric Template	Spiritual Plane	Crown	Accountability
Celestial Body		Third Eye	Equality
Etheric Template		Throat	Spiritual Responsibility
Astral Body	Astral Plane	Heart	Willingness to Change
Mental Body	Physical Plane	Solar Plexus	Presence
Emotional Body		Sacral	Authenticity
Etheric Body		Root/Base	Divine Will

Due to the nature of our body and the connection of the Spiritual Ethics Framework, we will begin with the pillars —Divine Will, Authenticity, Presence, Willingness to Change, Spiritual Responsibility, and Equality and Accountability—that help connect our body to the ethical principles needed when serving souls.

The pillars are a foundation we can use to build the principles for serving others and raising the frequency and vibration of Earth. They have been shared to help those souls who have been contracted for leadership, as healers, energy workers, or other spiritual workers, to understand the great responsibility of what we have been gifted.

Each aspect of the framework carries with it an energetic signature that can be connected to Mother Earth through the use of a crystal. Whilst there are many that you may feel resonate with the ethical principle you are focusing on, the crystals suggested are merely a guide. If you feel like using crystals in your practice as reminders of the Spiritual Ethics Framework and find a crystal that resonates with you more than the one suggested, please honor your intuition and use this crystal instead. Different crystals, as it is with humans and souls, carry different energy imprints. This may lead to you resonating more with one crystal than another. For example, whenever I use labradorite, it will fall off me or go missing. Alternatively, when I have tiger's eye, it tends to stay around for as long as it can. These are reflective of the energy in both my energetic field and that of the crystal.

Similarly to crystals, each aspect of the Spiritual Ethics framework carries an energetic signature that has a guardian or guide to assist you. This may be different depending on which aspects of the Universe you interact with. While there are infinite guides, we have been guided to choose a being from the Angelic/Buddhic plane, a spirit animal, and a plant ally. Again, as with the crystal described, if there are guides or guardians you are more affiliated with or feel more aligned with, use your discernment and encompass these beings into your practice. Alternatively, you may also be curious and feel pulled to research and discover more about the beings highlighted.

For example, if you prefer to serve using guidance from plant allies, Rose is more likely to govern the energy around the pillar, Willingness to Change, which is also connected to the heart chakra. However, if you work more with Angels and the Ascended Master, this same pillar may make you feel pulled to the energy of Jesus. Similarly, if you prefer to call upon Spirit Animals, the energy of this pillar may resonate with the magpie or the antelope. Again, trust what is right for you and what guardian or guide comes forward. There is no right or wrong in this aspect of work, but rather what is aligned to your heart and your intuition. You may choose not to explore this aspect of the Spiritual Ethics framework, and this is perfectly fine as well.

As you read through the Spiritual Ethics framework that has been provided by the Universe, there is a caveat to using your own discernment. If you would like to alter a practice, apply it a different way, or resonate with a different idea, this is what you do. You need to honor your intuition and treat this information as a guidepost and a basis for engaging intentions when serving different souls. This, in turn, will result in a practice that resonates with your soul, encompasses the spirit of the ethics being shared, and allows you to serve souls for their highest and greatest good.

Always come back to what aligns for you and use this book to bring into consciousness a more enlightened and awakened way of serving souls who have chosen to connect with you. Trust in yourself and hold yourself accountable with a high level of integrity and responsibility. Your intention when entering into work with others is the greatest indicator of how you will show up in the world.

For those of you beginning your spiritual journey or seeking a practitioner to guide you, do not be afraid to ask questions—and it is ok to expect honest answers. Be open and curious and find someone who is aiming to empower you, who sees you as someone who is whole and unique, and who allows you to feel comfortable as you are, especially if you are seeking healing. Seek a practitioner who leaves you feeling that you have changed and grown rather than less than or unworthy. Learn to trust your inner guidance and follow what the Universe has created for you.

CHAPTER 3 PILLAR 1: DIVINE WILL

The first pillar needed prior to engaging in any work is the understanding of Divine Will. If there is no understanding of this pillar, then a soul is not meant to be serving in this area. It is linked to our Freedom of Choice and is never to be compromised without the implications of karmic debt. This means that imposing on someone's Freedom of Choice can lead to lessons and contracts being created that follow the soul across multiple lifetimes until cleared.

When channeling, healing, or engaging with others, we are not there to judge or tell them what they may need to do, but rather just pass the information on and allow it to flow through. The information may reflect our lives or those we know, but it is not for us to interpret. Each soul has their own interpretation of information based on experiences in both this life and the past. It is very similar to the concept of interpreting dreams. A lake house might conjure great memories for someone who has parties there during the summer, but it might conjure poor memories for someone who has had a loved one die there. Try not to think, apply logic, or interfere with this process. It is important to stay clear and neutral. When serving each person, understand that there is nothing wrong with them and that they don't need to be fixed. They are whole, and we are here to serve them with the guidance and feedback we receive from the soul we are serving. We are just messengers and need to stay out of "ego," which can lead to judgment or the feeling of something needing to be fixed.

This leads to the premise behind Divine Will. Everyone has free will to choose. It is important to ask permission if the person wants to receive information as well as if they would like any messages from spirits who may have passed. Volunteering information, or seeing more than the soul is ready for, creates a level of disrespect both for ourselves and the soul we are serving. For ourselves, we are passing on messages or information without prior permission, which can negatively impact us. In turn, a soul receiving information they are not ready for can lead to them changing their path or missing life lessons which may result in their soul not being able to move forward. Interfering with Divine Will impacts the whole Universe and reflects the great responsibility placed on us.

Let me share an example. A soul comes and joins you for a session, asking for guidance and some healing. She has been married for nearly 20 years and is constantly losing her voice, suffering from lung infections, and having stomach issues. As you begin to receive information to guide the client, it becomes apparent that she is unhappy in her marriage, and you are shown what her life would be like should she choose to start a new relationship. However, this is not your judgment or decision to make. You may state and share observations and make suggestions for the soul to work on her health. You may even regale stories of how you experienced similar symptoms in your old relationships (if this is true— only speak honestly). You, as the practitioner, cannot interfere with the soul's Divine Will by saying she should leave her marriage. Or that her husband is horrible. Or whatever feelings or judgments may come through. This prevents the soul from coming to her own conclusions and influences her decision. It impacts her Divine Will. You are merely there to provide guidance for the highest and greatest good and hold a space where energy can be raised and messages can be shared.

A soul may be presented with information, and it is up to them how they act upon it. Some souls will ignore it and choose to stay in an infinite loop of trauma or stagnation in their spiritual development, as they are choosing not to change. It is important to remember this is perfectly ok. Some souls will act on the information and then decide it is too difficult, challenging, or overwhelming, and return to their previous pattern or frequency and thus return to old patterns and behaviors. This is perfectly ok, too. And then there are the souls who are courageous, the ones who are brave and understand the need to reclaim their power, heal the wounds, and choose to walk a higher path. This is also perfectly ok. The souls are all treated equally, respected in their right to choose and use their Divine Will, and not judged nor criticized for whatever choice they make.

You need to understand that we always have free choice. We can choose to live or die. We can choose to eat food that nourishes our body, mind, and soul or that drains our energy. We can choose to lead from our hearts or let our egos tell us how to live. We can choose to do the work and healing and move to a higher path or stay right where we are. These are all free for the soul to choose. This is the very essence that refers to Divine Will.

This is further encumbered when we consider how we work with others. We need to make a conscious choice to stop volunteering our aid to the souls we meet. You can share your story and what you are able to do; however, do not volunteer to help the person. This interferes with their Divine Will as you are not allowing them to come into their own power and choose to interact with your services. Most of you reading this are in the line of work that serves others, and we often have much to give. This can lead to temporary amnesia of the concept that a soul may not be open to your assistance at this part of their soul journey.

By volunteering to provide aid without their request, we are not respecting their Divine Will to choose, and in turn, we are not respecting their journey, ourselves, or our energy as we rush to volunteer to help. You, too, have a right to enact your Divine Will and choose not to serve a soul if they do not align with your energy. Use your discernment in this moment to determine what is aligned for you as much as them.

Let me also emphasize that volunteering does not include acts of service such as holding a door open, giving someone physical directions, aiding at soup kitchens, and so forth. These are comparatively acts of kindness from a place of service. However, these, too, should still be weighed to see if they are aligned with your soul or being completed out of obligation. There is a difference in energy fueling these services when coming from "want" versus "have to." The volunteering to aid includes your services, your inner wisdom and/or insight, or a different path you can sense for them.

We, as humans, have DNA that has been created from a place of polarity. As we all carry light and dark energy, or good and bad, it is important to remember that duality is needed for balance. This is directly linked with Divine Will and Freedom to Choose. Whilst you may be "fated" to walk a certain path, it does not occur unless you make the choices you need to get there. Similarly, you always have the power to change your destiny. This is why being human is such a unique and beautiful experience, as we learn to rediscover all elements of ourselves, to own shadows and triggers, and move into a place of love and light. This polarity makes humans unique and highlights the divine blueprint given to us by the Universe.

The Low of Divine Oneness

The Universe has 12 laws that govern how life flows and moves. These laws are the fundamental principles that govern all aspects of existence—physical, mental, emotional, and spiritual. Divine Will has been linked to the Law of Divine Oneness. The Law of Divine Oneness is based on the principle that everything is interconnected. Every thought, action, and event is connected to everything else. What we do to others, we do to ourselves. We are all connected and undivided. By observing everyone and allowing them to be, we are respecting the Law of Divine Oneness. The difficult part is learning not to be impacted by what others say, do, and/or feel and staying in our own vibration.

As we are all an image of the Universe, we can never be disconnected from each other. This has been proven through the holographic principle in quantum physics, where the tiniest particle is still influenced by its original connection even when separated. The term "boundaries" is one that many use. However, this will never be fully in existence due to the energetic nature of the human being. Standing in your truth will allow energy to shift and the "boundaries" to come into play. You will never be able to fully push other souls out of your life, but rather, as your energy shifts higher, they will no longer be attracted to your vibration. This leads to them "disappearing" as it flows with other universal laws, including the Law of Attraction, which is "like attracts like," and the "Law of Polarity," which is that everything has an opposite to provide contrast and create balance.

Returning to the Law of Divine Oneness, one can think of the rock in a pond to help create an understanding. Whilst the water, symbolizing us, is all peaceful and connected, it continues to be water together. However, when the rock, symbolizing an event, occurrence, or interaction, is thrown into the pond, the water is impacted. It is not one molecule of water that misses out on the impact of the rock, but every molecule. Some molecules will be more displaced than others, and some will barely move at all. However, in the end, the original state of the water has been changed, as it is all connected, just like the energy fields of humans.

If you are finding it difficult to comprehend, it is simply that we are all connected and, therefore, are impacted by each other's energies, decisions, and choices no matter where we are in this world. Being mindful of where you put your energy and how you spend it will ensure that you maximize your ability to exert your own Divine Will. It is through conscious choice and decisions that we are able to choose how we react to those around us.

Learning to Trust Your Intuition with Muscle Testing

My mentor taught me this simple process of muscle testing, and I have also seen it used by a number of other practitioners in various forms. It works using the principles of kinesiology and relying on feedback from our body to let us know if something is congruent (yes) or incongruent (no). You may prefer to use a pendulum if this is a method you are more comfortable with, and it is your Divine Will to make that decision.

We only use this method when there are no emotionally charged questions (e.g., don't ask if you should quit your job or sell your house). Also, remember to be hydrated and avoid using words like "don't," "isn't," "can't," and "not," as your mind finds this difficult to compute. If you want to test a "not" statement such as "I don't want chocolate," try asking "I want chocolate" and then see if you get the yes/no response.

There are several different ways to truth test, but these are the two main methods.

Method One: Fingers

1. Make sure you have had some water and are hydrated before starting this process.
2. Put your thumb and either your forefinger or ring finger together in a circle. Hold them together tightly.
3. Place your forefinger from your opposite hand on the circle and pull to make sure you are holding tight.
4. Say, "Soul, show me yes." Note if your fingers stay together or pull apart when you ask this.
5. Say, "Soul, show me no." This should be the opposite of your "yes" response.
6. Say, "I am a woman/man," depending on your gender, so you can see your body's response to this. You should get the "yes" response.
7. Now, try the opposite of the above to see your body's

response. You should get a "no" response.
8. Be true to yourself and ask some more questions that you know are true about you and are not to gain confidence in this process.

Method Two: Use Your Body

1. Make sure you have had some water and are hydrated before starting this process.
2. While standing (preferably facing north), place your arms crossed over your chest and close your eyes.
3. Say, "Soul, show me yes." Note if you move forward or backward when asking this.
4. Say, "Soul, show me no." This should be the opposite of your "yes" response.
5. Say, "I am a woman/man," depending on your gender, so you can see your body's response to this. You should get the "yes" response.
6. Now, try the opposite of the above to see your body's response. You should get a "no" response.
7. Be true to yourself and ask some more questions that you know are true about you and are not to gain confidence in this process.

If your body does not move, you may be dehydrated, so make sure you have had enough water

Once you have practiced these methods a few times, it can be used to establish a practice to gain trust back in yourself/intuition and reconnect with your soul. You can start with the following exercises to help you build confidence in your truth testing. If you can do these every day, it will help you to become more confident.

Exercise One: What do I wear?

Use your truth testing to help you pick out your outfit for the day. This can be underwear, clothing, and even jewelry. If you have to wear a uniform, it might be how you wear your hair or something you can change.

Exercise Two: What should I eat/drink?

Ask your soul what you should eat for a meal using the options you have available. It might be what you put on your toast, if you should have eggs or oatmeal, or my favorite is when going to a café and choosing something off the menu (it makes it so much faster).

Exercise Three: What should I watch/read?

Use your truth testing to help you choose something on TV to watch or what book you may want to read. Often, our soul knows just what we need, so let the truth testing guide you.

Root Chakra

It is no accident that Divine Will is linked to the root/base chakra. For this chakra, it is about the "I Am." Safety, security, identity, stability and feeling earthly all come from this point. When we have a clear understanding of our identity, it allows us to be clearer on the idea of our freedom to choose as in Divine Will. If we are not in a place of safety or stability, it can be difficult to translate the idea of always being able to choose. We will instead operate from fear of the unknown, from a place of anxiety and instability rather than anchoring in ourselves.

It is through this notion that as mentors, coaches, spiritual guides, body workers, and practitioners, we aim to create a safe space for guidance. As we hold space and support the soul in working through its pain, we need to be mindful not to make the choice for the soul who is engaging in our services and/or guidance. We must always allow the soul to choose, for it is through Divine Will that we master the art of accepting everyone on their journey —that we truly feel into the notion that all souls are whole, imperfectly perfect and exactly where they need to be. It is through Divine Will that the soul is able to become the change they want to see in their life. However, it is not up to us to make this decision for them; we are simply the vessel holding space to allow for divine communication and serving the body in this physical state.

Keeping a clear root chakra for yourself will ensure that you are grounded in your work. Many practitioners who engage with the Universe have a tendency to want to stay in this higher vibration or plane, and this is often where the feeling of peace is found. There is nothing wrong with this practice; in fact, it is encouraged as it strengthens your intuition and spiritual connection. However, you still require balance and, as such, need to ensure your lower chakras remain in tune and flowing.

Crystal Connections

The crystal which has been assigned to the pillar of Divine Will is obsidian. As stated earlier, you may have a different crystal that resonates for you in relation to Divine Will and the root chakra. Please trust your intuition and use what aligns for you.

Obsidian is created from molten lava that has not crystallized fully. Due to this alchemy, it carries many elemental energies and is a stone synonymous with not being limited or bounded in any way. This poetically mirrors the notion of Divine Will. Obsidian is a stone that grounds you and will deflect any negative energy so that you can exercise Divine Will without the influence of external energies.

Whilst there are many types of obsidian, the black obsidian tends to carry the purest representation of Divine Will. It is a stone that embraces the dark and yet still transmutes the light and allows the polarity of being human to be reflected in its creation. It is through Divine Will that the crystal can choose not to further crystalize and pause to capture the essence of the fire element and turn it into something powerful.

Guide or Guardian Connection

As mentioned, the guides and guardians described in relation to the pillar of Divine Will are based on energies that have been channeled through. If you have other guides or guardians who align more with the energies of the pillar of Divine Will, trust your intuition and discernment to evoke these energies. Alternatively, if you feel pulled to research the guides or guardians suggested, then allow that to happen.

The guardian who oversees the pillar of Divine Will is Goddess Kali. Goddess Kali is able to embrace both her shadow side and her light, the masculine and the feminine, and find the balance in between. Evoking the spirit of Kali will allow you to embody the ability to choose and respect each soul's Divine Will. Goddess Kali allows you to release your fears, overcome your limitations, manifest your dream, and connect with your divinity.

The animal guide aligned with the pillar of Divine Will is the elephant. Elephants remind us that an animal so strong and large has the power to create destruction whilst it is also gentle and compassionate. The elephant can choose how it wishes to react in situations and seeks a place of harmony and balance, just as the Divine Will reflects one always has a choice.

The plant ally allocated to the pillar of Divine Will is the eucalypts. As a eucalypt tree stands tall, it makes a choice to continue to grow and anchor its roots into the ground. It has a choice to provide shade and be home to animals, and it respects the choice of nature and the natural cycles of Mother Earth. The eucalypt is able to see the greater need for balance and finding the Divine Will in all aspects of nature.

Summary

Divine Will is respecting a soul's right to choose—to choose to remain on their path, to alter from their path, or to move onto a new path and timeline that raises their frequency and vibration to return to their divine blueprint blessed upon them from birth. It encompasses our own right to choose and emphasizes the need to accept the polarity of all aspects of life, including the darkest parts of ourselves. When you can allow an opportunity for the soul who you are serving to choose, the best outcomes for the highest and greatest good will occur.

This pillar of Divine Will is important for an understanding of working with ourselves and also how to work with those souls who choose your guidance. With an understanding of being connected, it also highlights the need for authenticity, which is the next pillar of life. Through being authentic, we are able to truly show up in this world.

CHAPTER 4 PILLAR 2: AUTHENTICITY

The pillar of Authenticity is vital in any offerings that you have to serve on Earth. It is a term that, in recent years, has been used as a mask for what a person is truly feeling or being. True authenticity comes from a place of vulnerability. It comes from your heart when you are clear on who you are and in alignment with your standards and values, which stem from knowing and understanding your soul's purpose.

As a human first and foremost, you are always learning. Your vision may change and expand as you reach higher levels of consciousness and switch timelines. This does not mean your soul purpose, values, or standards should shift. At times, this means standing in your truth when those around you are afraid to or do not understand the message. We are fortunate to be living in a time when the healer, the witch, the soul, or the light worker is not asked to dim their light for their own personal safety. Rather, it is a time when we can be free to truly express who we are as souls incarnated on planet Earth and be part of the greater awakening.

Karmic wounds will often restrict those who have been harmed for shining their light in this life, in generations past, and even through past/parallel lives in our soul fragments. To understand the impact this has, let me share an example from my own karmic wound.

I have been a healer for many lifetimes over. This has often led to persecution, burning at the stake, and other atrocities for my soul gifts did not comply with the societal norm, or in some cases, did not provide darker souled individuals to get the gains they wanted over others. One such reincarnation resulted in my soul choosing to serve as a midwife. I had a deep and thorough understanding of herbs, which allowed me to create tonics, elixirs, and compresses for women in the birthing process and resulted in many improved outcomes, less pain, and, most importantly, less death. The doctors who I worked with at the time did not like my connection with nature. This was not from a place of knowing better but rather from a place of the ego. They started to whisper that I was a witch, and secretly, I was what one might refer to as a green witch. I was deeply in tune with how others felt, as well as the magic and abundance of healing medicine nature has to share with us.

I felt a shift in my workplace, which deeply saddened me as I was serving by assisting with the wondrous miracle that is known as birthing a child. The emotions and tension grew, and it resulted in me becoming a hermit, living in a small cottage in the middle of the forest. I could not share my knowledge or wisdom due to fear of further repercussions, and my being knew it was unsafe to do so. Further events led to this being confirmed and resulted in my death.

This wound of anger and fear was transferred to me in this life. This soul fragment was genuinely concerned for my safety and for sharing my knowledge and connection with nature and the world. It took many sessions and clearing to address this karma so that my soul could authentically express itself, still from a place of vulnerability, but without the encompassing fear of safety for my life.

Many of us are likely to be carrying such wounds, and it is important work to clear these. They may not be clear, but as they come up, it is integral to do the healing practices needed to shift, release, or integrate these old soul fragments so that you can authentically express yourself from a feeling of safety. Not feeling safe leads to motivations that can cloud you from being open to authentically showing yourself to the world. In turn, we choose to apply mask after mask to hide who we truly are. This energy of hiding prevents you from shining your light and authenticity. It also hinders your ability to serve others and may come across as a mismatch of energy.

Emotional Awareness

The core of Authenticity is to be aware of your emotions, to be able to tap into your sacral chakra, and to be strong enough to let your ego move to the side. To complete and master this work when healing, guiding, and/or mentoring souls, it is important for you to be aware of your flaws and triggers to prevent these from limiting your ability to discern for the soul who has elected to work with you. You need to have an awareness and ability to let go of your ego pain and any wounding from the past in this life, parallel or previous.

For example, a soul may come into your sacred space and leave their shoes in the middle of the doorway where you step down. For an unknown reason, this causes you to feel the soul is irresponsible and can cause harm to others. You have no other reason for this apart from where they left their shoes. As you explore this judgment and feeling, you discover that as a child, you left your shoes in the doorway, which led to your mother stepping on them and spraining her ankle, and in turn, you were roused upon for your behavior. It is by recognizing and clearing this trigger that you can come from a more authentic space.

Whilst at times this may be difficult to do in the moment, you are always able to exercise your Divine Will and choose to request help. Ask your spirit team or the Universe to clear the immediate emotions and show you the issue has been solved and resolved. This does not mean it has been fully shifted, and deeper work should be contemplated. However, it will allow you to return to a place of Authenticity and be free from the emotional triggers and judgment that arose from the simple action or word, such as placing shoes in the middle of a doorway.

It is important to heal any aspects that come to light and ensure that you continue to clear out any emotions, old beliefs, opinions, judgments, or patterns that may arise. Our soul is continuously healing, clearing out the cobwebs and the fragments that may impact our ability to be an empty vessel when intuiting for others—this includes all levels of work on the mind, body, and soul. When we hold onto these old patterns, emotions, beliefs, opinions, or judgments, it impacts our ability to lead and takes away our ability to be a conduit of the Universe and serve the soul who has chosen to grace us with their openness to engage our service.

Ego vs. Intuition

Often, we create identities/roles that we put ourselves into. For example, you may call yourself a "healer," a "medium," or a "psychic" to help others understand what you do. Whilst most people need this to feel comfortable with who they/you are, it limits you and your capacity to heal. This is important as we are often beyond what our certificates and degrees label us. Furthermore, further study for such areas should be done to fill a void in your curiosity rather than to say you are that qualification. Your ego is your identity that is influenced by spiritual beliefs and ideas that shape us, including titles. The ego has a knack for making these beliefs, ideas, and qualifications as a sense of superiority and entitlement rather than vehicles assisting you in your practice. Ego is what drives the need for a soul to have a certain title in order to believe they are worthy or superior when contrasted with others. In comparison, intuition can pick up on the genuine energy of the person and single out who is authentic and on their soul path versus someone who is misaligned.

We need to remember to stay present and move from our authentic selves on a soul level. When we remember that we are a vessel of information being exchanged for the highest good, the ego does not have a chance to be involved. When we move from our soul essence, it does not require a level, but it is just in the service for the highest good of all involved.

Authenticity needs to be encompassed in every aspect of your life. You cannot receive or share information whilst serving others and then not carry this out yourself. This is the basis of the expression "phony," which is used to label someone who is not incorporating the information they have received into their life. Reflecting and incorporating the information you learn or that is passed through channels helps raise your own vibration and the vibration of those you interact with.

Heart Connection Meditation

To be able to live authentically and listen to your intuition, you need to connect to your heart. It is through listening to our heart and the wisdom that comes from within that we are able to authentically express our true desires and soul purpose.

It is important to make time to connect to your heart and listen to the wisdom it has as part of your regular spiritual practice. By trusting the messages that are shared from your heart, you are then able to get clarity on moving forward and living as your authentic self.

The following is a guideline for a heart connection meditation that you may wish to encompass into your spiritual tuning and for guidance. It should take around five to ten minutes.

1. Find a quiet space and close your eyes, focusing on your breath. Breathe in through your nose and out through your mouth.
2. After several breaths, after you breathe in, hold your breath for a slow count of four before letting your breath out again. Repeat this process for five cycles.
3. On your next breath, feel the air going into your heart

space. You may wish to place your hands on your heart to help you connect with this energy.
4. As you continue to breathe into your heart, ask yourself, "What is my heart's greatest desire?" and trust whatever wisdom comes forward. You may like to vary this question to what you need right now, what you need to know, or whatever message you feel pulled to ask your heart.
5. As you get the message and wisdom, slowly open your eyes and give gratitude for the message your heart and soul have shared.

Sacral Chakra

The pillar of Authenticity is linked to your sacral chakra and emotional body. This is by divine design, as when we are honest with our feelings and emotions, our authentic expression can be radiated. We can create and establish connections with others whilst being able to express our true desires. When our sacral chakra and/or emotional body is imbalanced, our authentic self finds it difficult to radiate through. This highlights the importance of being self-aware of our own energies to limit our impression of others when not being truly authentic.

As mentioned earlier, being aware of your triggers and flaws that radiate from this area can be a powerful tool in shifting to a place of authenticity. For example, if you find it difficult to move through doubt or the feeling of being worthy, addressing these feelings that arise from the sacral chakra can lead you to find more authenticity in all that you do without the need to question your intuition or the wisdom that you have to share with the world.

Crystal Connections

The crystal that has been assigned to the pillar of Authenticity is amber. As stated earlier, you may have a different crystal that resonates for you in relation to Authenticity and the sacral chakra. Please trust your intuition and use what aligns for you.

Amber is a crystal created from the fossilized resin of ancient trees. It carries with it a Universal wisdom from being entwined in the network of Mother Earth whilst being connected to the energy of the tree it was part of. Amber's wisdom, as with obsidian, allows the deflection of negative emotions. However, unlike obsidian, it transmutes these negative emotions into positive emotions and removes blockages that stop the flow in our bodies.

Its beautiful color varies between yellow, orange, and brown, which in turn reflects its authentic nature. This is captured in the crystal of amber and can be transmuted throughout the energy of its use.

Guide or Guardian Connection

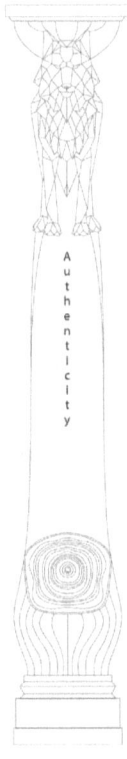

The guides and guardians linked to Authenticity are based on channeled energies. If you have other guides or guardians who align more with the energies of the pillar of Authenticity, trust your intuition and discernment to evoke these energies. Alternatively, if you feel pulled to research the guides or guardians suggested, then allow that to happen, too.

The guardian who oversees the pillar of Authenticity is Goddess Freya. Her ability to authentically express herself and be true allows others to radiate in her presence. Goddess Freya is sensual and allows her ability to connect with magic, curiosity, wonderment, and animals to guide her as she shows her true nature with the world.

The animal guide aligned with the pillar of Authenticity is the wolf. Wolf reminds us to look into our hearts and check our authentic selves. It reminds us to be true to ourselves and to stop pretending to be something we are not. The wolf is here to allow you to align with who you are meant to be.

The plant ally allocated to the pillar of Authenticity is sandalwood. Sandalwood allows you to gain control of your emotions and, in turn, express your authentic self. It brings about a calm and serene energy whilst opening your heart and balancing your ego. Trees themselves dig in their roots and stand tall to reach the heavens, authentically themselves and perfect just as they are. Sandalwood encompasses the energy of Authenticity and the sacral chakra whilst in a balanced state.

Summary

In summary, Authenticity is an integral pillar that can be channeled into all aspects of your life. Being vulnerable and open whilst remaining aware of your limitations and own beliefs empowers you to be the conduit you need to be to share wisdom, heal, and guide. By choosing to come back to your heart and setting an intention that everything is for the highest and greatest good for all involved, then you are able to move from an authentic place. Be clear on your values and standards, your flaws and beliefs, and move from your heart so you can truly be authentic.

In order to embody the energy of authenticity, there is a need for our soul to learn presence. When we are truly present in the moment, it assists us in embodying our authentic self as well as the intuition our heart provides us to guide us when serving souls. This leads us to our next pillar, "Presence."

CHAPTER 5 PILLAR 3: PRESENCE

The spiritual ethics pillar of Presence is one that allows you to act from a place of neutrality. It allows you to be in this place of neutrality by embodying the practice you have chosen to use as a vessel to serve the world. It is in the current moment that we are not influenced by the past or the future. There is no regret or worry. No angst or anxiety. Rather, you are simply present to receive the inner wisdom of what allows you to serve the souls you work with. This pillar builds upon our understanding of Divine Will and Authenticity, as without the other two elements, it is difficult to be present. Our mind/ego will often overtake our true soul purpose, and practicing Divine Will prevents us from judging whilst also listening to our intuition from our heart.

Being present also allows you to honor your own standards and values. If you are not clear on what this means, this would be a great initial practice for any soul to complete. Your standards are what you expect of yourself and others in terms of actions and the words used. If you are not honoring your own standards and being clear about what these are for yourself, how can you expect others to honor and abide by them? This, too, goes for your values. Your values are what you need to encompass your vision—what you embody when serving the world, what you seek in this world to move further. This, in turn, creates a practice in your life that allows you to align with your purpose and vision and create a set of non-negotiables that form a pillar of who you are.

For example, you may have a standard of acting on your intuition as soon as it happens. You share this with others and encourage them to do the same. This comes with values of connection and courage. In turn, this leads to a non-negotiable practice of connecting with your spirit team each day and being clear on your intuition and guidance.

However, you find that you start to compromise your standards and values, as the intuition you received will be triggering to yourself and others. Instead of trusting the guidance, you choose to put it in a drawer and push it to the side. As a result, you do not embody the message and standard of acting on your intuition for yourself and find yourself missing opportunities and disappointing yourself by not upholding this standard, which then, instead of allowing yourself to be authentic and present, results in you portraying a mismatched energy. This makes it difficult to serve souls as you are not honoring yourself fully, so how can you honor them?

Being in Presence allows you to move from a place where your ego cannot surface. The ego is there to process what is happening in the moment and only comments when we let our awareness travel forward or backward to project into the past or future. It is this art of being still in the current moment that allows the soul to express itself fully.

If you find it difficult to be present, the art of the breath is a practice that will reengage you in the here and now. By tapping in and noticing your breathing, the movement of your chest, the beat of your heart, and feeling into your body, you can return to the present moment and be fully connected with your body. This is why breathwork is a growing area of interest for those in self-development. It is when we are fully in our bodies that we can let go and allow the flow and creativity of the Universe to wash over our lives.

Again, this is a practice we should complete to foster relationships with others. Whether it is with family, friends, colleagues, or clients, being fully present is necessary for meaningful relationships. Too much emphasis has been placed on having a relationship with the devices given to us, and we often forget to look up and see the soul right in front of us. Practicing presence helps us shift relationships and allow more authenticity. These pillars—Presence and Authenticity—work together to build deeper connections between souls.

Nature and Presence

When searching for examples of how to be present, we need to take a moment to reflect on nature. As you sit under a tree, on a rock, or in the sand, your energy is immediately grounded. We are present in the moment as we engage our senses in what is happening around us, with no agenda but to observe, sense, and wonder in the beauty that surrounds us. This is how a soul can be fully present in the moment.

Learning from the trees that help us to breathe is another practice to remind us of presence. Their roots are deeply embedded in Mother Earth, which we can liken to being clear with our standards and values. The tree continues to grow and reach for the heavens above and the sun to share its magnificence in the world. It knows it has strong roots. It knows it can move with the wind and the weather, flow with the ups and downs in its life, and trust what is coming. The tree is simply present in the moment, accepting of what comes and knowing the Universe and its Divine timing will come as needed.

We have many lessons and practices we can learn from being in nature. A yoga practice called "The Magic of Mouna" allows us to simply sit and observe. This can be accomplished by choosing a place in nature that you sit and observe each day. The timing is up to you, but I've found sitting for at least ten minutes allows for the most magic to happen. By doing this with the same spot each day, you will notice changes, whether it be the leaves of the tree, the animals that arrive, or even simply the sky. It allows you to be present and observe the magic that nature has to offer to reinstall a feeling of curiosity and wonder within us. It is through these feelings that you can truly understand the pillar of Presence and the alchemy that stirs from a place of stillness.

We can take the observation of nature into solving problems that arise in our lives. However, problems are there for us to learn and grow, and it is important to remember that it is not meant to be encumbering but rather a lesson. When working through a problem, it does not matter what aspect of life this is regarding; there is a need to be present on what is happening. When our attention is present on the obstacle we are facing and we detach ourselves from the outcome as well as the cause, we can see a new angle that needs to cause the shift or solution needed. It is by being present in the problem, without judgment or expectations, that the solution often presents itself, and our intuition can guide us without the influence of the ego.

This phenomenon often happens when you have an ongoing problem and choose to take a break. You reset, come back into yourself, and breathe. This may be from going for a walk, having a shower, or whatever practice takes you out of the emotions of what will happen if this isn't solved. It is from this state, when we have come back into our bodies and can be present again with ourselves, that the solutions usually arise.

Grounding Practices

These simple grounding practices can be used when you are unable to walk barefoot upon the Earth or before serving a soul/s in your practice. If you have your own adaptations, you may wish to use these instead, and as always, these are here to provide you with a guide.

Connection Meditation

1. Start by closing your eyes and just breathing in through your nose and out through your mouth (if you can).

2. Feel your sit bones in the chair and your feet on the Earth.
3. Imagine your feet are sinking into the floor beneath you, pushing further down.
4. Feel or imagine vines or cords connecting you deep into the heart of Mother Earth, making you feel earthed and grounded.
5. Slowly open your eyes when you are ready and wiggle your fingers and toes.

Light meditation

1. Start by closing your eyes and just breathing in through your nose and out through your mouth (if you can).
2. Feel your sit bones in the chair and your feet on the Earth.
3. Imagine a beautiful, colored light (whatever is right for you) coming in from the top of your head.
4. Feel or imagine the light moving down the back of your head, through your spine, down your legs, and out your feet.
5. Feel or imagine the light continuing to move into the Earth, reaching the very center.
6. Feel or imagine the light now coming back up, back through your body, and out the top of your head. You might like to imagine this as a circle forming around you.
7. Slowly open your eyes when you are ready and wiggle your fingers and toes.

Solar Plexus Chakra

The pillar of presence is connected to our solar plexus and the mental body in our auric field. It is the last pillar connected to the physical plane of existence, for being present is part of the human body experience. Choosing to be in our body is integral to the practice of presence.

The solar plexus is our power center and where the sense of self-worth originates from. When stepping into the energy of the solar plexus, we have no choice but to be present. Present with ourselves and the creativity that lies within that allows us to do what we need to in this life. Our confidence and ability to execute and create in this plane comes from the solar plexus and being present.

This directly ties into the mental body. Our thoughts are shaped by the energy we are portraying in our body, mind, and soul. For example, if you believe a conversation is going to go badly, your body and mind will start reacting this way before you are even in the conversation. Instead of listening to the person you are speaking with, you default to searching for reasons to support the thought that the conversation is going badly and subconsciously close your body off by crossing your arms or holding a passive facial expression. However, when choosing presence, you listen and engage in what is being shared rather than entertaining the projections, what-ifs, or worries that have been construed from belief systems or traumas from the past. When you are present and in the moment, the mental body has no choice but to also be present. These counteracting beliefs and past experiences have no bearing on the conversation that is occurring. The mental body will try to move forward or backward out of the moment, but when we return to presence, then this no longer has any weight.

Decisions and Energy

The decisions that we make are just decisions. They are not here to define our lives, to be reconsidered, relived, or replayed on repeat until our ego can make a story out of what occurred. Your decision is true for you in the present moment. It is a yes or no. A maybe will take your energy and drain you, leaving you in a state of either past or future and not in one of presence. Any decision you make is perfectly aligned with you in the present moment.

Should your decision lead to a failure, setback, mistake, or "messing things up," you make the next decision and then the next to change, learn, and grow from the experience. By staying present and knowing your values and standards, as well as your vision, you are able to embrace the energy of making decisions that align for you faster and more immediately— and, in turn, make the next decision to move from what does not yield the desired results. Evoke the energy of Presence to assist you in moving forward and making decisions in all aspects of your life.

Crystal Connection

The crystal assigned to the pillar of Presence is Citrine. As stated earlier, you may have a different crystal that resonates for you in relation to Presence and the solar plexus chakra. Please trust your intuition and use what aligns for you.

With its warm color that has been compared to sunshine, Citrine brings a sense of joy and stillness that allows emotions to shift, confidence to rise, and a sense of Presence to flow in. It assists in motivating you and, in turn, allows you to persevere through problems. When taking the time to stare at the intricacies of Citrine, you can note the multiple facets that remind us of sunshine. The color itself comes from the heat of a volcano, again emphasizing the physical plane of the solar plexus, the connection with being present in your body, and the relationship with Mother Earth.

Guide or Guardian Connection

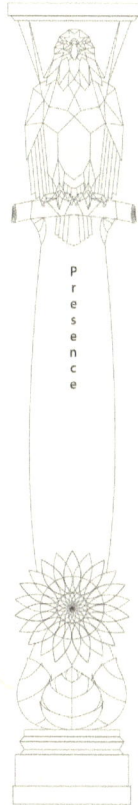

As mentioned, the guides and guardians described in relation to the pillar of Presence are based on energies that have been channeled through. If you have other guides or guardians who align more with the energies of the pillar of Presence, trust your intuition and discernment to evoke these energies. Alternatively, if you feel pulled to research the guides or guardians suggested, then allow that to happen, too.

The guardian who oversees the pillar of Presence is the God Ra. Ra, in Egyptian culture, was known as the king of the gods who oversaw creation. He chooses each day to battle to allow the sun to shine and watches over the flow of life. Ra is able to embody the gift of presence by reminding us to live life to the fullest and be grateful for the moment we have. Ra reminds us to free ourselves from the constraints that take away our power and allow us to triumph and move forward in our journey.

The animal guide aligned with the pillar of Presence is the eagle. The eagle is able to fly high and take things in from a higher perspective. He can sit in the moment and feel all that is happening around and below him without needing to account for what might be or what came before. The energy of the eagle reminds us to act in the greatest good after seeing what is right for us at that moment in time. The eagle allows us to connect with ourselves and the Universe and find what we need to move forward without discounting what is happening for us in the moment.

The plant ally allocated to the pillar of Presence is the sunflower. With its radiant and bright color, the sunflower reminds us of its Presence by simply being. It follows the sun and continues to shine its light even though it moves throughout the day. The sunflower opens itself fully and embraces the moment of light as it knows it is its time to shine. It is unwavering when coming up to challenges and stays true to itself in the moment. You can call on the sunflower to bring more joy, optimism, and warmth into your life and remind you to stay present.

Summary

The summary of Presence is being fully engaged in the present moment without consideration of past or future events and without exploring alternate outcomes. It is the act of being in the energy that is presented in front of you. This allows for authentic connection, aligned decisions, connections with nature, and the ability to create from a place of divine inspiration and empower ourselves and others. It allows you to be authentic in the current moment without beliefs, unconscious patterns, or trauma playing a role in influencing the outcome of the situation. Presence is an essential practice for all souls, whether serving others or not.

When we enact the guidance of Presence, we allow ourselves to open up to new possibilities and opportunities. Taking away the impact of the ego, the traumas and beliefs of the past, and the worries of the future opens our souls to greater opportunities for change and for new ideas and concepts that align. This leads us to the next pillar, "Willingness to Change."

CHAPTER 6 PILLAR 4: WILLINGNESS TO CHANGE

Life is not a straight line. In fact, it can take many turns, re-turns, and sidetracks in order for us to get to where we are meant to be on our soul path. Our soul evolves and changes over time based on the information we have collected through learning in this plane and intuition. However, when one becomes fixated on a set of beliefs or ideas and refuses to acknowledge or discern new information, it prevents our soul's ability to grow and evolve. This is why the pillar of "Willingness to Change" is needed when factoring in ethical principles for us to follow. The impact of each of the pillars we have explored thus far is important, as it reminds us that with Divine Will, Authenticity, and Presence, we can be more discerning and open to change. Divine Will reminds us that we are all connected and have a right to choose, Authenticity highlights the need for us to choose for our soul's purpose, and Presence reminds us to let the current moment be the guide as to our feel to change.

As much as our life is evolving and changing, so are those souls around us. Information that may have been previously true can change, and a new truth or set of principles, standards, values, or beliefs may emerge. This includes how we react to criticism. Being open to others' criticism and/or point of view allows for soul growth and evolution. This does not always mean that we change our core beliefs. However, feeling or reacting to a point of view reflects that there is a stirring of emotions within you. When we have our emotions stirred, it is an opportunity to heal and be open to change.

Using these times to heal assists with your ability to broaden perceptions and let go of anything that may be tethering you. It is a chance to reflect, discern, and adjust to any information that changes what you know. We, as human souls, are doing our best with what we know at the time that we know it. The power of wisdom and knowledge comes from a Willingness to Change when new information that aligns is presented to us. At times, this may rock our core values and beliefs, and it is important to discern whether this is the path forward.

One such example is water. How much water to drink has been an interesting topic that continues to be channeled through for clients and myself. Initially, I believed that I only needed around eight glasses of water a day. This was my base standard, and it was one I practiced. However, upon receiving a new intuitive download and information, I realized that this was not nearly enough for my body to detox the pollution we are exposed to every day, nor charge my cells to receive further integration.

From this intuitive information, I changed my practice and noticed a significant change in my body. It felt lighter, it was easier to detox, and I improved my ability to channel. Whilst this seems like an easy thing to change, I receive a lot of pushback from clients about this practice when it comes through as guidance. It is up to them to decide whether they want to change this aspect of themselves and return a soul's Willingness to Change.

Owning Your Field

"Willingness to Change" also extends to our energy and those souls who we permit to be in our field. This includes those who are physically present as well as those who we consume through scrolling and digestion of information virtually. This also includes social media, the news, the radio, and music. As your soul grows, you will notice a distinct shift in who you wish to permit to be in your field. This includes relationships, family dynamics, and what your soul is able to digest from external input.

Being open to changing your relationships, as well as what you expose yourself to, can assist in protecting your energy and permit more rapid growth in your practice. When you remain in the old energy, it becomes a tether and anchor that prevents you from moving forward. It interrupts your ability to express your authenticity as well as your presence to the new evidence or opportunities being shared. The old energy limits you from seeing how your energy is being impacted in the moment and whether this aligns with your soul.

This does not mean you need to leave a marriage, dissolve a partnership, or disown your family. Rather, it is where you choose to have deep conversations about your soul's new vision and/or desires and how this can be furthered together rather than apart. Sometimes, this may lead to a dissolving of the old relationships. And sometimes, it leads to a more powerful bond and dynamic that inspires those around you. Either outcome cannot be measured as good or bad. In contrast, it is a measure of your willingness to change, and being open to the new energy coming through can result in a greater dynamic or openness to something new to assist you on your journey.

As a soul who may be seeking a practitioner, you do not need to feel loyalty to whomever you initially choose. As you grow on your journey, you may or may not continue to be challenged to grow by your practitioner, and then it is time to use your intuition and discernment if it is time for a change. Be open and curious, honor what is right for you, and the practitioner should come from a place of understanding that your journeys are no longer entwined as closely, if at all.

For example, I met my naturopath in my early twenties. He helped me work through many emotional layers using Neuro Emotional

Technique. He unpacked my health issues and supported me through the end of my first marriage, the end of my business partnership, the stress of running companies, growing and having a baby, and selling my last allied health practice. I went from regular weekly appointments to fortnightly to monthly to just pop in to get supplements. I will make an appointment sporadically and have moved to other forms of energy to work with my health. This is not to say that if I feel pulled to make an appointment, I should refrain from doing so. We have mutual respect, and we have assisted each other, and he has served me through the most dramatic changes of my life. He is not angry that I no longer hold a standing appointment and accepts that I will see him when I feel pulled to. We are both open to the change in our relationship, as he assisted me. I learned from him and am grateful, and I would like to think he also learned from me as we reflected our journeys in life to each other.

It was through our relationship that I learned and grew in my understanding of emotions, meridians, and the body. That I finally understood how my body would feel when running low on certain supplements, and that I was also open to changing and becoming less dependent on someone for my health. It was his wisdom that opened me to being curious to take control of my health and body, to listen to the messages, and to be less fearful of change. Interestingly, it was also through him that I met Carli, my spiritual mentor.

As this practitioner-client relationship changed and evolved, so did we. We do not hold each other in poor regard as we do not see each other as regularly, nor do we hinder each other's growth. We were both willing to change the dynamics of our relationship and the support we needed at the time.

As a practitioner, it is important to remember this change in dynamic. Empowering the soul you are serving to step out and find their own path in life is an amazing reflection on you. If you are a body worker, it is the satisfaction that the soul chooses to listen to your advice, complete the exercises, and turn to you from a place of trust when their body is not working how it should. You may also feel pulled away from a certain type of soul as you grow on your journey, and these souls will fall away from you. This is not necessarily a reflection of you not serving them, but rather them no longer serving you. Being open and willing to allow this change to occur will help shift your energy and attract clients who are more aligned with you.

I personally experienced this when moving out of allied health. As my soul continued to grow and my vision for life shifted, the clients I served began to fall away due to moving out of the area, finishing their therapy journey, changing circumstances, or other reasons. I, too, felt myself being pulled away from the profession and was open and willing for the change to occur.

Sitting back and observing those who come and go from our lives reflects what our soul needs at the time. Of whom we need to be surrounded to allow our souls to change and grow. Be open and willing to flow with these changes and allow your frequency to continue to elevate as you move through life.

Tips for a Powerful Conversation

Learning the act of deep listening and embodying this in your interactions can support your practice of Willingness to Change. It is through deep listening that you can hear, feel, and see what is truly occurring for you and the soul you are conversing with. The idea of a powerful conversation is to address difficulties in relationships and allow for the opportunity for all parties to "win."

The tips for ensuring you are using deep listening, as well as the soul you are conversing with, include:

- Set up a time with no distractions and the pretense of having a conversation about the issue you wish to discuss

- Allow each soul to clearly share and express fully, with no interruptions, what they need to say.
- Whilst the other person is speaking, repeat in your head what they say and listen. Do not plan to respond. You are simply being present and listening.
- Repeat back to the soul the main messages conveyed to get clarity.
- Once the messages are clearly defined, the other soul can speak with the same expectation of no interruptions and being listened to, with the main message repeated.
- The conversation should end with all parties coming away with a clear way forward—a win-win situation with no one feeling unheard, unseen, or unfelt.

Heart Chakra

A Willingness to Change is associated with the heart chakra as well as the astral plane. It is the connection between the spiritual and physical plane. Through the heart, you can be open to love, compassion, empathy, and forgiveness. It is through forgiveness that we allow ourselves to grow as souls as well as in connection with others. It is through the heart that we can also connect to the universal truth of our soul and trust that if we choose to change, it is for our highest and greatest good.

There has been much evidence to show that the heart acts as its own portal, bringing in and pushing out energy into the Universe. It is by no accident of design that in the middle of our being, we are also creating a divine connection with those around us, Mother Earth below us, and the Universe above us. Our heart is the conduit between all aspects of the body, mind, and soul, as well as nature, humanity, and the spirit realm. It is essential that we are true to ourselves in the initial pillars to build certainty so when information, whether intuited, spoken, or other, comes into our field, our heart will know whether this will influence us in needing to change or stay within our core beliefs, standards and values.

The magic of heart knowing, or cardiognosis, allows logic to be surpassed and enter more into a place of love and attraction to what is rightly aligned. It is an intelligence that comes directly from the Universe and, at times, will not always make sense to those around you. Rather, trusting this guidance and intuition is where the magic of the Universe will be allowed to flow through you.

A tree, whilst appearing solid, will still manage to bend with the wind and move so it does not break. This is like being open to change. When you want to change, it does not mean that you break down all the beliefs you have built up, but rather, some may need to bend and adjust to the new conditions. When we know no better, we are able to forgive ourselves and stay where we are. When we do know better and continue to choose not to change, our growth as a soul will be halted.

The heart chakra also encompasses a lot of the emotions and energies that allow one to serve souls in the world. The emotions of love, compassion, empathy, and forgiveness all come from the heart. These emotions also encompass the energy of the pillar of Willingness to Change. It is through understanding and forgiveness that emotions and energy can be alchemized and released in order for someone to grow. Learning how to forgive the unforgivable assists in returning to your power and shifts trauma and wounds that echo throughout lifetimes. The power from tapping into this space allows your energy to resonate with that of divine love from the Universe and, in turn, may be used to serve souls.

Crystal Connection

The crystal assigned to the pillar of Willingness to Change is rose quartz. As stated earlier, you may have a different crystal that resonates for you in relation to Willingness to Change and the heart chakra. Please trust your intuition and use what aligns for you.

Rose quartz encompasses the energy of love. This includes love for yourself and love for others, as well as the concept of "being in love." It allows you to accept your perceived flaws and befriend your fears and doubts from a place of love. In essence, rose quartz reflects our imperfectly perfect nature and the beauty of being open to love and a Willingness to Change. The beauty and essence of being in your heart space are linked to the energy of rose quartz and, in turn, being open to the love and guidance that is in tune with your divine expression and Willingness to Change.

Guide or Guardian Connection

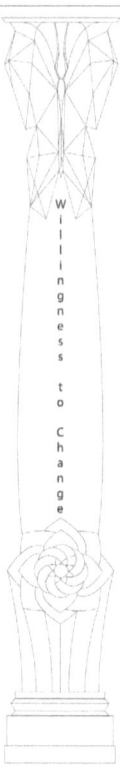

As mentioned, the guides and guardians described in relation to the pillar of Willingness to Change are based on energies that have been channeled through. If you have other guides or guardians who align more with the energies of the pillar of Willingness to Change, trust your intuition and discernment to evoke these energies. Alternatively, if you feel pulled to research the guides or guardians suggested, then allow that to happen, too.

The guardian who oversees the pillar of Willingness to Change is Jesus, or Yeshua. Yeshua was the embodiment of unconditional love. He helps us connect to our heart space and reminds us to be open and caring towards other souls. Yeshua treated everyone equally and would hear their story, feel their pain or allow them the space to be. He never forced his opinion or belief onto anyone and rather chose to move from a place of love. Throughout his time, Yeshua was open and willing to change and learn to enhance his practices whilst staying true to his standards and values for himself at the same time. He did this without judgment or prejudice and from a place of love.

The animal guide aligned with the pillar of Willingness to Change is the butterfly. Just as a butterfly knows when it is a caterpillar that it will be undergoing a great metamorphism, it does not know what is coming on the other side, and yet there is still a willingness to change. The caterpillar turning into a butterfly is a miracle of nature, and yet the butterfly, once it reaches this stage, knows it needs to change and embrace this new life it has transformed into. Some butterflies do not even eat; rather, they embark on what it takes to continue their lineage and allow the next generation to experience the willingness to change and undergo transformation.

The plant ally allocated to the pillar of Willingness to Change is the rose. Rose is a beautiful and sensual diva who shows her ability to move from a bud to an expression of sacred geometry with petals layered upon each other. It emanates a soul emerging and continually being open to change as each petal of the rose represents a changing part of our soul. She shares her beauty and changes her expression slightly with each season based on the feedback from the soil, the weather, and the water available to her whilst still being her loving rose self. We are able to emulate the Willingness to Change based on the information we share and by being strong in our standards and values moving forward.

Summary

In summary, a Willingness to Change is essential to allow your soul, gifts, and skills to grow and evolve. As new information is presented or opportunities arise, it is our duty to check for heart alignment. This is the time when we need to surpass logic (e.g., our mind and ego) and tap into our cardiognosis to discern if this information or opportunity is aligned with our soul. Trusting in your heart and being stable with your core values is essential when entering into this work and serving others. This allows you and those you serve to continually evolve and shine as the blessing the Universe knows you are.

The pillar of Willingness to Change created a pathway for the next pillar, Spiritual Responsibility. For if we remain stagnant and never choose to evolve our soul, we are compromising our soul's growth. It is one of our responsibilities to be willing to change in order to provide the best practice that aligns with our soul and those that we are serving.

CHAPTER 7 PILLAR 5: SPIRITUAL RESPONSIBILITY

When a soul chooses to seek out a shift in their body, mind, or soul journey, there is a level of responsibility for all the parties involved. Souls who are seeking assistance are in a vulnerable state, and they are looking at us for answers to be healed, to be guided to their next step, or to have their energy shifted. They may feel that they are in judgment or carry a feeling of being incomplete, not whole, or even being less than others. It is our Spiritual Responsibility to ensure that any exchange we have is fair, equal, of the truth, and with the intention of the highest and greatest good for all involved.

Our exchange needs to reflect this level of responsibility to see all as equal and as a direct reflection of us. By staying present and moving in authenticity, we speak or move with the divine flowing through us. The words and the information we share need to be from a place of the highest guidance for all involved.

We need to be aware of the power of what we say, and the energy we can shift is beyond what we can recognize, as it can lead to powerful healing or, in polarity, destruction. We need to ensure the words we say are pure and in line with the divine. That the energy we move through the body is meant to be shifted and freed without hindering the lesson or emotional pattern that needs to be learned for the soul receiving the treatment.

What we say can impact the future of the person we are serving. As we learned in the earlier pillars, a soul always has free will. It is also of great importance to ensure that any information shared does not interfere with the soul contracts or life lessons attached to the soul. This creates a state of events for the soul that limits growth and prevents the soul from achieving its reincarnation goals. For example, saying to a client, "By quitting your job and moving to the south coast, you will meet the love of your life," has different levels of concern. Firstly, you are providing an absolute of what we say—there is no other path or option; rather, it is "If you do this, then this will happen."

Secondly, it might also prevent the soul with whom you share this information from forging a clear path. They may also miss out on other lessons. We do not know what will happen if the person quits their job, as they might not be able to move to the coast due to making other choices. All parties in one's future timeline involve Divine Will and, therefore, will never be set in stone. For this scenario, a statement such as "If you choose to explore leaving your job, other opportunities may arise; however, it is for you to decide" places the power back in the hands of the soul you are serving. Therefore, you are honoring the information coming through by providing it as a possible opportunity rather than an absolute. This allows the soul you are serving to make a choice to honor their Divine Will, their Authenticity, and their Willingness to Change, and you have merely provided them with an option that may not have previously been considered. There is no karmic consequence for either soul.

To help the process, you can set an intention for the work you are aligned with. This may include highlighting your purpose to align with the greater good for _all_ involved. You may also wish to emphasize that the information can change and that it should not be absoluted. For example, the following may be used, with your own discernment, when choosing to connect with a soul's higher self and/or spirit guides:

"The intention of this channel/ energy work and session is for the highest and greatest good for all involved. That the information shared is of the highest vibration for (person's name) and that it is correct for this current moment in time."

The soul who has chosen to work with you should be made aware that the information shared is true for the moment. That is, timelines constantly shift and change based on the choices souls make and the karma being attracted to the soul. One such example is when a person chooses to wait and hold the door open in an elevator for someone they see coming. That momentary decision could change the path for the person holding the door (we shall call them Person A) and for the person running for the lift (we shall call them Person B). Should Person A have chosen not to hold the lift, they would have run into a person holding a coffee, which then spilled down their shirt, which, in turn, meant they were late and looked harried at an important meeting, which led to a series of events including missing out on his promotion. However, because Person A decided to hold open the lift and wait, he did not run into the person, made his meeting on time, and gave an excellent presentation that resulted in his promotion and more abundance in his life.

Alternatively, Person B was able to make his appointment on time by not having to wait on the lift. This meant he was able to regain custody of his child and allow her to come out of a difficult situation. If he missed the lift and was late, this would have been marked against him and delayed the custody process, and, in turn, led to his daughter suffering.

Whilst it was a simple act of kindness holding open the elevator door, it led to different choices and actions being taken by both Person A and Person B—hence creating new timelines and outcomes for the soul on its journey.

As such, when giving a soul information or completing bodywork, we are sharing what is best to improve the outcome and assist the soul in creating the change they are ready to receive. We cannot give them too much as they may become overwhelmed or change their trajectory from being in a state that is not yet receptive to shifting to a more aligned or higher path. Our life is a journey, and when rushed, souls who do not yet have all the information will feel pulled further back rather than accelerated. Some rare souls will grab onto the higher timeline and quantum leap; however, this depends on the anchors in the old identity that may be holding them behind.

Another example is something that occurred during a channel for one of my clients. I was shown the outcome of the soul's highest timeline through which making one decision would lead to the soul finding their soul mate, their dream place to live, and a fulfilling job that uplifts them each day. I could not tell them what the choice was, as they still had lessons to learn and beliefs to shift. It was my Spiritual Responsibility in this moment to ensure I only conveyed the information needed for the soul to reflect on their life and make the choice aligned for them in the moment. I could not share the information as this would have changed his current trajectory and may also have resulted in the timeline not being fulfilled due to choices being made before divine timing allowed for it.

For those of you who are body workers, would you release underlying trauma without first clearing a pathway to it? Would you not ensure that each movement you made or bit of energy you imparted was not for the highest good of the soul entrusting their body with you? You would first address the initial issue and work up to the deeper underlying difficulty once there was a higher level of trust and a better knowing of the soul's body. As each body is unique, both physically and energetically, it is important to retune yourself each session to ensure the energy you put into the body is for the highest and greatest good for both you and them.

This is what is meant by sharing information that is correct for the moment. It is our Spiritual Responsibility to take care with the words we use and the practices we utilize in our sessions. In turn, this does not mean that any information shared, practices completed, or healing offered will be fully entwined in the soul's life. It is the soul's Spiritual Responsibility to choose to act upon what was shared or given. The Universe can only leave so many breadcrumbs for a soul to follow before it chooses the path that is right for them in that moment.

Spiritual Hygiene

As a practitioner, you also have additional responsibilities. Creating a sacred space where the soul you are serving feels safe is integral. This is to ensure energies are aligned, that the space is neutral, and that you are not influencing the outcome in any way. There are no strict guidelines for creating a sacred space, but rather, there are intentions that should be kept when setting up your space. These include:

- Clearing the energy of the space so it is neutral
- Allowing the soul who comes to feel warm and welcome
- The space creates a feeling of safety where one can be vulnerable if they choose to be
- The space is created for the highest and greatest good of all souls within it
- At the completion of the session, the space is closed, and the energy is discharged for both the soul being served and the practitioner

You may wish to contain your space using crystals, runes, grids, calling in ancestors, guides, plants, animals, and celestial beings. It does not matter how you create this container; it is just necessary to ensure the best shift possible for the body, mind, and soul. Trust your intuition and guidance as to which practice is right for you.

Additionally, it is your Spiritual Responsibility to continue with your own healing journey. Being human means we have endless layers of healing that need to be cleared. It is a continuous journey. As you continue to expand and shift into higher timelines, you will have a resurgence of old patterns, beliefs, or triggers that you felt were previously addressed. This is no mistake; it is the Universe working to clear out cobwebs and allow you to step into your greatness and highest divine blueprint. It is the magic of choosing to shift these patterns, beliefs, and triggers that has an impact for all the generations before and those to come after. Again, this emphasizes the importance of this Spiritual Responsibility.

When serving a soul, it is often the case that we attract those who are experiencing similar issues to what is in our lives. This is due to the Universal Law of "Like Attracts Like." This may lead to energies arising during your practice. In this moment, as you are anchored in presence, it is important to shift and not pass on these energies to your client. If you are triggered, heal your own emotions there and then so you do not move from it. It is imperative that you return as quickly as you can to a place of neutrality, and it is your responsibility to ensure this does not impact the information being shared, whether verbally, through body work, or spiritually. This is an additional responsibility to holding a sacred space.

In addition to healing in the moment, as with the sacred space, it is also important to clear your field regularly and live in the wisdom that comes from within. This keeps you in alignment and allows you to create a clear channel for the energy of the highest and greatest good. Auric field clearing is an important practice and can be performed using whatever method resonates with you. It may be through tuning forks, colored balls of light, calling in angels, or even spirit alliances. The methodology does not matter. It is the intention of the practice that is integral and part of your Spiritual Responsibility to ensure your energy is neutral and prevent any transference of energies to the souls you are serving.

Finally, we also need to establish good closing practices. At the end of each session, we need to zip up our own energy as well as the soul who has chosen to come to us. This prevents any lingering energy exchange. You may have your own practices for disconnecting from the energy of the client, and, again, the method is not important, but the intention with which you complete the action is. Once the soul has left the sacred space, the final act of spiritual hygiene is to reset the space. This may be done through incantations, smudging, white light washing—whatever method resonates with you. It is stressed to have a solid intention of bringing the space back to a neutral vessel where further healing, guidance, or practices can continue without any impact from the previous energy shift.

This, too, applies to distance work, particularly over a device. Simply disconnecting from the session does not mean the space has been closed. You would continue to clear your space the same way and may even use additional practices to assist in shifting the energy from the device used for the connection. This process can be as simple as placing a crystal that absorbs negative energy on the device, such as smoky quartz, selenite, or shungite, and then cleansing the crystal afterward. You might use white or gold light clearing, smudge around the computer, or call in your spiritual team. The method does not matter—it is the intention of neutralizing the energy in order to allow for a place of neutrality and to wipe any energetic imprints that may influence the next soul who works with you.

Your Own Protection

As much as a practitioner is responsible for their own energy and creating a sacred space, they can also take action to protect their own energy when seeking ways to work with others. There are a number of practices that you can embrace or research further in regard to ensuring your energy is protected as you seek out practitioners to serve you. These following practices can be used according to your own discernment.

1. Smudging

Smudging is a time old tradition that involves using a plant to help change the energy in a space. It engages all four elements —Earth and water are represented by the herb/plant you choose, and air and fire are represented by the burning part. It is known as a purifying ceremony that is used to shift energy and protect the energy you want to keep.

When choosing a plant to use for smudging, you may wish to investigate the cultural implications as well as the sustainability of the plant you are using. Use your discernment on what feels right for you—and this may change depending on the energy you are trying to shift. Some herbs you can use are sage, palo santo, eucalyptus, rosemary, lavender, cedar, juniper, mugwort, or peppermint. Different herbs contain different energy and can be used based on your intention to clear your energy or the space.

2. Amulets

Amulets can be created to help us stay protected. They help deflect any energy we no longer need but also can keep in or protect the energy we want in our lives. They have been used for centuries to help the wearer bring "good luck" and change the energy they need. The following ritual can help you program your amulet as well as allow it to continue to protect and deflect energies for you.

1. Choose a crystal or piece of jewelry you already have and then put it on selenite to clear it.

2. Once you feel the energy is open, place one hand on Mother Earth and one of the piece of jewelry/crystal whilst saying: *"I command that this necklace (or whatever you have chosen) become an amulet of protection and invisibility. That it may serve the greater good and any energies that are not of the highest frequency be transmuted in love and light and returned to where it came from. Thank you, Mother Earth/Gaia, for helping keep us grounded and using your energy to support us."*

3. Then change hands but raise your hand that was on the jewelry/crystal to the sky. Now say, *"I command that those trying to project on me be reverted back to the sender whilst receiving love and higher frequencies in return. We ask that spirit helps guide you to higher planes and that anything no longer mine be transmuted in love and light. Thank you, spirit for helping us stay connected and remembering who we are."*

4. Now, put both hands on your heart while holding the piece of jewelry/crystal in between. Then state, *"With this amulet, I am protected. I am invisible. This amulet is created to protect me for the highest and greatest good so my soul may continue on its journey. We ask that any time the powers infused are needed, it is of the highest and greatest good. Thank you. Thank you. Thank you. So be it, so be it, so be it."*

This can also be done for all household members by just having them in your intention when charging the amulet. Instead of saying "myself," say their name.

You also need to practice daily cleansing of the amulet by placing it next to quartz (not selenite, as it will reset it). But you can then put the clearing quartz on selenite to clear it when it feels full.

3. Shields

When you think of shields, you might envision a knight with a shield fighting off a dragon or even a forcefield being put around a spaceship. It is not far off how shields work energetically, but instead of a physical shield, we use light/energy to help repel what we do not want in our lives. Shielding practices include pulling in your aura to constrict or expand your energy field; cloaking yourself through visualizing a cloak, a hoop pulling your energy in, or even a special forcefield; calling in your spirit team such as Archangel Michael or the plant diva for mugwort; using crystals such as tiger's eye, black tourmaline, shungite, selenite, labradorite, or quartz; using light runes that you can energetically paint around where you are or onto a piece of jewelry; pulling in white or colored light through your chakras and your auric field as well as to ground and anchor our energy.

These are just some practices, and you can create one that is unique to you. Trust what you feel pulled to and research different methods that align. You may ask other practitioners you work with, and they might also provide you with insights.

Throat Chakra

The art of Spiritual Responsibility is linked to the throat chakra and, in turn, the Etheric Template in the auric field. Our throat chakra is linked to our vocation as well as to our authentic expression. Similarly, Spiritual Responsibility is expressing the will of the Universe in whatever practice you have chosen and doing so from a place of presence and authenticity.

The throat chakra may become stagnant if the information shared is not of the highest and greatest good. Similarly, there have been experiences where those who are hearing information that is untrue for either themselves or the soul they are serving can lead to a block in the throat chakra and may result in the words not coming out clearly or being "choked" by the energy. This can become clearer and more pronounced through your spiritual hygiene practices, which allow you to discern whether the information or energy conveyed is from a place of integrity.

The Etheric Template stores the energy reflection of what occurs in the physical body. Again, participating in spiritual hygiene will ensure that the energy being conveyed in the session is not influenced by experiences that are occurring for you. It is important not to pass on any energy or symptoms. It is your Spiritual Responsibility to take every measure to ensure this does not happen. It is always your intent that will lead to this practice becoming more succinct and automatic. The transference of energy usually occurs for the more sensitive souls who have yet to tap into their ability to contain their own energy.

Crystal Connection

The crystal that has been assigned to the pillar of Spiritual Responsibility is aquamarine As stated earlier, you may have a different crystal that resonates for you in relation to Spiritual Responsibility and the throat chakra. Please trust your intuition and use what aligns for you.

Aquamarine is a stone of courage and calming energies that allow for your true, authentic expression. It encourages you to serve humanity and to link into a higher level of consciousness that can be utilized when encompassing the pillar of Spiritual Responsibility. It assists in clearing the throat chakra with the Universe's energy and, in turn, taps into a greater wisdom than what can be purveyed through logic. The balance of aquamarine supports communication, brings out your courage, and allows you to learn and evolve your practices to ensure how you are serving others is for the highest and greatest good.

Guide or Guardian Connection

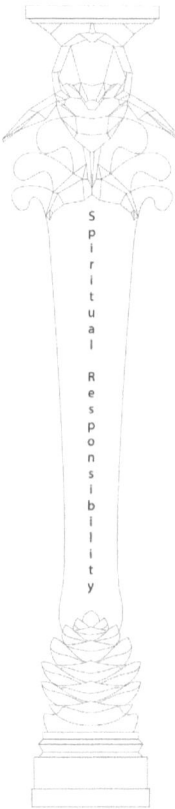

As mentioned, the guides and guardians described in relation to the pillar of Spiritual Responsibility are based on energies that have been channeled through. If you have other guides or guardians who align more with the energies of the pillar of Spiritual Responsibility, trust your intuition and discernment to evoke these energies. Alternatively, if you feel pulled to research the guides or guardians suggested, then allow that to happen, too.

The guardian who oversees the pillar of Spiritual Responsibility is Archangel Bath Kol. She is known as the divine daughter of voice and assists you with your ability to love, create, seek, and speak with greater clarity, as well as sing out what you want in the world. Bath Kol will allow you to choose words and create actions and practices that align with the highest Spiritual Responsibility.

The animal guide aligned with the pillar of Spiritual Responsibility is the dolphin. The dolphin is known for its playful nature, intellect, and ability to work in pods or alone. The dolphin is linked to Spiritual Responsibility as our words carry a frequency that impacts everything around us. The dolphin reminds you to create community and self-love whilst communicating effectively. Call on the dolphin when you need assistance with your Spiritual Responsibility.

The plant ally allocated to the pillar of Spiritual Responsibility is pine. Pine stands tall and overlooks the forest around it, knowing that it is at peace and still protecting. Its sap is medicinal as much as its leaves, and its personality focuses on harmony and looking after those around it, much like the essence of Spiritual Responsibility. Pine will allow you to protect whilst also allowing your true self to be present.

Summary

In summary, Spiritual Responsibility encompasses the practices you use to look after yourself energetically as well as those souls who choose to work with you. It is essential that all practitioners establish excellent spiritual hygiene practices in order to ensure they are working from a space of neutrality. It does not matter what modality you are working from; this is needed to ensure that no energy is transferred between souls at any level. In addition, it is imperative that you are mindful of your words, actions, and practices and ensure they are for the highest and greatest good for all involved.

The pillar of Spiritual Responsibility allows us to begin to move into the next pillar—the pillar of Equality. As much as we are responsible for the practices and information we share with the souls who choose to engage our services, we also need to see them as our equals. Equality is as much as a Spiritual Responsibility as being aware of your own energy.

CHAPTER 8 PILLAR 6: EQUALITY

The pillar of Equality is as its name describes. We are all equal and connected. There is no hierarchy, no levels of someone being higher than another, as in the end, we are all souls created from the essence of the Universe and contain the same spark as each other. Those souls who you serve are there to be empowered and treated as your equal, with an exchange of energy. This may be through money, time, practices, knowledge, a hug, or even a heartfelt thank you. In the end, we as souls all have something to share and are valued exactly as we are.

Those souls who come before us to engage in the practices we use to serve are a direct reflection of ourselves. This reflection can lead to triggers and emotions being activated in us, which is why it is important to engage in your spiritual hygiene practices. How many times have you learned a new practice or information to share, only to find a soul placed in front of you almost immediately who needs that practice or information? How often have you found yourself unpacking a life situation, and, in turn, all the souls you work with have similar experiences? This highlights how we are all connected and is the essence underlying the pillar of Equality.

We are not better than another soul due to our position in society, our collection of degrees, or our life experiences. All of these aspects only represent a different sharing you have to offer the world. It is important to rebalance the energy or belief that if someone is seeking your service, you hold a position higher than them. We are all equal and can learn just as much from each other.

To put this in perspective, I would like you to imagine a politician and a cleaner who cleans his home. From the outside, they appear to have very different lives. They have different goals, income brackets, and living situations. However, in the eyes of the Universe, these souls are equal. In fact, these souls have similar fears of not being heard, not being able to provide for their families, and feeling they need to find a way to help others in the world. These souls, whilst having different ways of serving, are equal and are to be treated as such. And even if they did not echo the struggles of each other, they are still human beings with souls that live through multiple lifetimes and experience death as the end of each cycle. They are souls that need nourishment and love. They are souls that need food and water to survive. When stripped down to the soul essence, we are all equal, connected, and the same.

All Is One

In all aspects of our service and connection with spirit guides, celestial beings, and the Universe, we are all equal, as all is one. Just as we create a feeling of equality with the souls who choose to engage our services, this flows onto our interactions with the different beings we interact with for guidance, messages, and assistance in our human form. The Universe sees us all as equal. Likewise, any soul is able to connect and speak to the Universe directly and will be treated as equal.

If you find this difficult to understand, it starts with the remembrance that we reflect our spirit guides at some point in time. It is by no accident that we and they have chosen to form a soul contract with us. Rather, it reflects the guides who resonated and chose to serve us on our soul journey. "God" and humans are equal, and we need to keep this in mind to help us return to wholeness/oneness. It is a notion that has been lost through the centuries and one that separates us from our infinite and connected nature of who we are in our soul essence. When you are able to accept that we are created in the image of the Universe and, therefore, are equal, it gives you some insight into the power and infinite possibilities we, as souls in this incarnation, can access.

Energy Exchange

Through this connectedness, we need to consider that everything is energy. We, as those chosen to serve a soul with their body, mind, or spirit journey, need to account for equality through an equal and fair energy exchange. In our current world, this may be in the form of money. However, it can extend to the bartering of services or goods, the exchange of kind words, or even a hug. There will be times when you may attract those who wish to use your service without this equal and fair exchange. Before considering saying yes, contemplate the following questions:

- Are both souls gaining equally from the exchange?
- Is one soul giving more than the other? This does not equate to fairness or equality.
- Are you, as the one serving, compromising your standards to accommodate the soul who wants to use your service?
- Do you both feel your energy is the same or increased after a session?

These are important to help you align with your worth as well as your abundance of energy. When we choose not to honor ourselves and compromise our values, this is going to magnify a scarcity energy with the Universe and result in attracting less into our lives. Again, it is important to be clear in your values and standards and befriend your flaws and triggers so you are able to honor yourself. Remember, you are a blessing and are here to bless others with your gifts of service.

If you are a soul seeking a practitioner, then it is also important to feel that you are receiving what you expected. Having clear expectations by both you and the practitioner you have chosen is necessary for ensuring you are both receiving a fair exchange of energy. Being able to ask questions and be comfortable with expressing what you would like out of the session are commendable starting points for choosing the right practitioner for you.

Field Clearing Meditation

This simple meditation can be used to clear your field as you continue to shift who you are in life. It was shared with me by a friend, and I loved its simple nature. This can be done each night before you go to bed, after you have had a heavy energy/emotional interaction, or whenever you feel you want to clear your field.

A field is your energetic boundary, how far your energy spreads. When we interact with others, the energy in our field shifts. As everything comes in a polarity, this can shift it into a higher vibration or frequency or a lower one. When you are open to change, this can lead to your field's energy shifting. Your field's energy may need to be rebalanced to align with the new information you are ready to integrate.

In order to complete this meditation:

1. Sit or lie in a comfortable and quiet space.
2. Close your eyes and take a few deep breaths in through your nose and out through your mouth.
3. As you settle into your body, imagine or visualize yourself in a field—there may be flowers, animals, and lots of grass. Trust whatever is right for you.
4. As you look on the ground, you will notice a circle of rocks around you.
5. Note if there are any people, animals, energies, or beings inside this circle with you. These all need to be removed to the outside of your circle. This includes loved ones and children; they can stay close but need to be outside of the circle.

6. As you clear the inside of your circle, pull in a beautiful, colored light. The light is going to flood the circle and everything around you.
7. When you are ready, take one more deep breath and then open your eyes. You have completed the meditation.

Third Eye Chakra

The pillar of equality is linked to the third eye chakra. The third eye chakra encompasses opening to new vision and learning to trust your intuition and inner wisdom. It is the basis for insight and imagination, and when linked to the pillar of equality, it allows us to see that we are all equal, connected, and created in the image of the Universe. It is through this inner wisdom and knowing that we are able to see each soul as a reflection of ourselves and the Universe.

The third eye may become restricted when questioning one's value or role in a relationship. Again, this is where the idea of an equal and fair exchange comes to light. If you are in a relationship or exchange of energy that does not align, and you choose not to see this, it can lead to a feeling of confusion, skepticism, and a lack of clarity as we ignore our inner wisdom and intuition. We can also find an imbalance when we energetically choose not to see an event, relationship, or situation for the energy and representation it is and put our intuition in a drawer. The more we choose to suppress our intuition, the more numb we become. We disconnect from our feelings of being equal with others and, in turn, our ability to trust our inner wisdom.

The third eye chakra is linked to the Celestial Body in our auric field. The Celestial Body allows us to be open to choices, enact decisions, and balance the energies for an opportunity presented to us. It is through this auric field that you are able to tap into your spirituality and awareness and receive guidance from higher planes. This is also important for encouraging a practice of equality as it allows you to feel what a balanced energy is for you.

Crystal Connection

The crystal assigned to the pillar of Equality is amethyst. As stated earlier, you may have a different crystal that resonates for you in relation to Equality and the third eye chakra. Please trust your intuition and use what aligns for you.

Amethyst, with its purple hues, encourages a high level of spiritual awareness and is beneficial for opening up one's third eye as well as one's ability to trust one's intuition. It helps balance high and low energies and brings an energy of equality. In addition, amethyst assists one with cleansing energies and allows for true connection with oneself.

Guide or Guardian Connection

As mentioned, the guides and guardians described in relation to the pillar of Equality are based on energies that have been channeled through. If you have other guides or guardians who align more with the energies of the pillar of Equality, trust your intuition and discernment to evoke these energies. Alternatively, if you feel pulled to research the guides or guardians suggested, then allow that to happen, too.

The guardian who oversees the pillar of Equality is Saint Germain. Synonymous with the violet flame, Saint Germain expands your ability to tap into unconditional love and, in turn, your ability to see all souls as equal. He stands ready to help everybody in their endeavors and does not discriminate against anyone. Saint Germain helps alchemize fear and create freedom, which allows you to connect with the Universe and understand that we all have the same birthright to happiness, irrespective of our status or position in life.

The animal guide aligned with the pillar of Equality is the emu. The emu is a bird that cannot fly, yet its size and long legs make it the biggest and fastest bird in Australia. It stands tall and allows itself to see its surroundings. Emu never takes things or people for granted and sees everyone as equal. He encompasses the energy of gratitude whilst also providing direction and support. He allows you to bring more focus into your life by seeing what is clear for your purpose.

The plant ally allocated to the pillar of Equality is the lotus. In Hindu tradition, the lotus is a sacred flower connected to different chakras as well as a symbol of balance and harmony. Lotus allows for equality by bringing forth a desire to self-actualize and support your path of consciousness. Lotus supports each chakra and allows you to integrate the messages equally when surrendering yourself to her energy.

Summary

The pillar of Equality is summarized as an understanding that all beings and souls you collaborate with are equal to you. You are no better or less than another soul, nor should we ever be made to feel this way by those we serve or collaborate with. It is important to ensure that when serving another soul, there is an equal and fair exchange of energy that honors and respects both or all souls involved. Similarly, if engaging the service of a practitioner, it is important for you to be open and clear on what you expect and that you are able to reflect on if it aligns with you whilst feeling equal in the transaction of energy. The pillar of Equality is linked to the third eye chakra and the need to honor your intuition. When you are clear with yourself, you are able to see that we are all connected to the Universe and are equally loved.

The pillar of Equality reminds us that we are all equal. This reminder is pertinent as we move into the final pillar of Accountability. By remembering that we are equal, we can also hold ourselves accountable for our actions as we serve other souls.

CHAPTER 9 PILLAR 7: ACCOUNTABILITY

The pillar of Accountability ties into the energy of Spiritual Responsibility as well as Divine Will. Everything we say and do carries an energy that can have irrevocable consequences should it be miscommunicated or misused. This includes how one conducts themselves in all aspects of their life. You are accountable for your actions, your words, and your energy, as well as how this interacts with others. Being the last pillar, it requires many of the pillars before it to support the practice of Accountability.

Again, there is an emphasis on continuing to be accountable for your own energy and healing work. We, as humans, are forever journeying to raise our vibration and, as such, continue to have misperceptions within ourselves that shake up aspects that need to be healed. When serving a soul, you need to be accountable for your words and actions by ensuring that you clear the way for them and do not create new cords or attachments that can be carried into their and your karmic field. This, too, carries into your everyday discussions, as you are accountable for yourself and healing to keep you aligned with Divine Will.

For example, a soul chooses to come to you in order to gain insight into their relationship difficulties. As you serve them and address their energy body, you can see a cord (an energy that represents an attachment between two souls) that is preventing the soul from shifting out of their current pattern of relationships, which is often detrimental to them. Without asking, you energetically remove this cord that is binding them in this relationship, and they continue on their journey, feeling a change but not understanding what it is. But they are grateful and then continue on with their life.

Now, this might sound amazing; however, this cord was a life lesson that the soul chose to overcome and work through in this incarnation. By the practitioner cutting the cord without asking permission or seeking more information if they were able to remove the cord, a new karmic template was created for both souls. The practitioner has taken away the soul's ability to further their soul development, and this, in turn, has led to them missing out on lessons that may lead to further healing in their life and will need to be repeated in their next incarnation. Furthermore, the lesson that you took away from the soul you are serving will attach to your soul as a karmic debt that needs to be balanced in the next incarnation.

It is crucial to ask for permission from the soul you are serving and, if working in the spiritual realm, from their spiritual team. If you are unsure, seek further clarification and make yourself accountable for setting up good practices to ensure there are no karmic repercussions. Additionally, should you do this in error, it is difficult to correct and rebalance.

In my own work, I have found when you engage an energy body and have clear intentions and practices, you cannot cut the cord accidentally. You may feel this is not for you, and you can further clarify this information with your or the soul's spirit team. It is very difficult to remove a cord that is attached to a lesson when you have engaged in the energy of the highest and greatest good for all souls involved. Furthermore, you can ask for additional guidance on how the cord can be shifted. You may be told it is not time yet, and this is ok. I have found it is often the soul's choice whether they are ready to remove this cord and you are able to guide them to do so. In some cases, you may need to provide assistance, and you will feel and be guided to what is right in the moment. Regardless of your guidance and actions, you are accountable for the actions you take or choose not to, based on the guidance from the Universe. This sole responsibility comes back to you and your practices.

Confidentiality

It should go without saying that all information shared in the sacred space you have created remains in that space. You may wish to share a story of a soul to inspire others, but this is where you respect their privacy and remove their name, as well as any information that may be connected back to them before doing so. It is vitally important that any soul who chooses to engage in your services feels they are in a safe place and can be open and vulnerable. This is not something to be taken lightly. Rather, it is a principle of which you are fully accountable.

Any testimonials or reviews should be shared with explicit permission from the person and, better yet, published by themselves. They need to be true, and you can hold yourself accountable for any feedback you receive. Negative feedback can be used as a chance to reflect on yourself and where you are on your journey, as well as a chance to grow. This is also the opportunity for deep conversation and listening to allow you as a practitioner to engage in feedback that can help evolve your practice. Even if the feedback feels misaligned, it is a chance for you to check what is happening internally for you and your emotions.

You may wish to keep records of your appointments, and how these records are kept will be reflective of your scope of practice. Again, it is important to ensure this information is kept confidential and stored in a manner that only you, or those serving with you, are able to access. Use your own discernment on how this would look like a best practice for you.

Karmic Rebalance

When choosing as a soul to be in service to humanity, the karmic effects of our service flow onto impacting and raising the frequency of the world as a whole. As each soul chooses to move to a high frequency or expand their consciousness, an equal reflection occurs for the greater good of Mother Earth. This is likewise true for souls that choose to dim their light and move to a lower frequency; this, in turn, lowers the frequency of Mother Earth. We need to remain accountable for this.

As discussed earlier, there is also a need to be accountable for our own karma. Continuing to heal and shift through your own healing and loving the "worst" parts of yourself will ensure your own karmic balance is restored and clear for the next incarnation. It is your responsibility to remain accountable for your own healing and to continue to raise your frequency when working with your soul and the future souls who choose to engage your services.

As a soul incarnated on Earth, healing is continuous and multi-layered. One lesson may have several recurrences. This does not reflect you "failed" or were "incomplete" in finishing the lesson from your first healing experience. On the contrary, as you rise to new levels of vibrations, energy, and frequencies, old patterns and wounds will re-emerge with a new focus for you to love, a new aspect you may not have been ready to consider and are now prepared to address. You are always seen as whole in the eyes of the Universe, and it is your choice to embrace your healing as a part of what makes you unique and able to shift the karma that has been weighing on your soul. Trust in your journey, in the greater good you cannot see, and give gratitude at the moment for these insights, lessons, and shifts in all aspects of your soul journey.

Ho'opoponono

Ho'oponopono is an ancient Hawaiian practice focused on forgiveness, reconciliation, and restoring balance within oneself and in relationships. This practice ties into the pillar of Accountability as it assists with reclaiming one's power and releases any attachments from past relationships whilst dispelling karma. The process involves introspection, taking responsibility for negative thoughts or actions, and using a specific healing mantra to cleanse and transform these energies into positive healing. It emphasizes the need to heal oneself as well as heal relationships with others to assist with Accountability.

The practice is centered around repeating a four-phrase mantra with intention and heartfelt sincerity:

- **"I'm sorry"**: Acknowledge and take responsibility for any harm or negative energy, including within yourself.
- **"Please forgive me"**: Ask for forgiveness, often directed toward oneself or a higher spirit, to open the way for self-forgiveness and healing.
- **"Thank you"**: Express gratitude for the healing and transformation taking place.
- **"I love you"**: Affirm love for yourself and others, reinforcing connection and compassion.

You can try this for yourself through a simple meditation as follows:

1. Sit in a quiet place and just breathe in deeply. Focus on breathing in and out, letting go of anything that doesn't belong.
2. As you are breathing, close your eyes and see or imagine the person/event you would like to let go of.
3. See or imagine wrapping up or putting in a box everything that happened to you. It might be words said to you, actions taken against you, or something that made you feel unloved. Once it is in there, return these to the person/event whilst saying the Ho'oponopono prayer:

I'm sorry

Please forgive me
I just want to say thank you
I love you

4. I sometimes add in "this is not mine" whilst returning the box. You may feel like giving many boxes or just one. It does not matter as it is whatever is right for you.
5. If you feel like doing so, you can call in other people/events to repeat this process.
6. When you feel you have returned everything with love, you can open your eyes and breathe out, knowing this has shifted.

Crown Chakra

The pillar of Accountability is connected to our crown chakra. Being the last pillar, it is connected to the crown chakra due to the emphasis on spiritual awareness, bliss, and feelings of enlightenment. It is about being accountable for your soul's energy and those you work with, in addition to the need to remain balanced in your body and with your connection with the Universe.

When the crown chakra becomes stagnant, a soul can become close-minded, confused, in constant frustration, or even continually seek a spiritual solution for an issue that is occurring in one's life. It causes a shift of power as you begin to believe the Universe will save you rather than having the power to save yourself. The Universe will move with you, but you still need to take the first step. Keeping your crown chakra in alignment is part of your accountability and also ensures you have a clear connection with the Universe.

The crown chakra and the pillar of Authenticity are linked to the Causal Body/Ketheric Template in the auric field. This energy is what allows us to connect with spirits and the Universe. In addition, it will broadcast any spiritual decisions, which, in turn, leads to energies and events shifting in our lives. Finally, at this level, you are able to energetically connect with soul fragments (parts of your soul that have been displaced and not reclaimed through lifetimes or interactions with other souls), which is where the karmic debt can shift should you not maintain your spiritual practices and accountability.

Crystal Connection

The crystal that has been assigned to the pillar of Accountability is clear quartz. As stated earlier, you may have a different crystal that resonates for you in relation to Accountability and the crown chakra. Please trust your intuition and use what aligns for you.

Clear quartz is known as the master healer. Its structure and properties allow it to hold multiple energies, and the magic of its balancing effects assists in amplifying energies for the highest and greatest good. Clear quartz is able to tune your soul gifts to have a great spiritual purpose and serves to align us with our minds by using more positive self-talk. The nature of clear quartz allows you to set intentions and, in turn, can be used as a pillar of Accountability when aligning with the highest and greatest good.

Guide or Guardian Connection

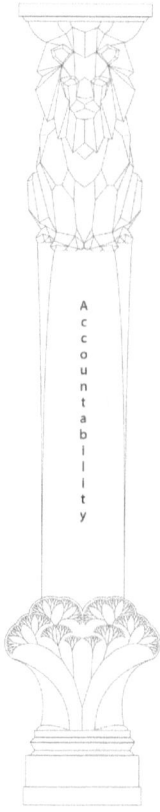

As mentioned, the guides and guardians described in relation to the pillar of Accountability are based on energies that have been channeled through. If you have other guides or guardians who align more with the energies of the pillar of Divine Will, trust your intuition and discernment to evoke these energies. Alternatively, if you feel pulled to research the guides or guardians suggested, then allow that to happen, too.

The guardian who oversees the pillar of Accountability is Ascended Master White Matthew. Ascended Master White

Matthew reminds us to own our power, individually and collectively, whilst standing in our divine presence from a place of love. He allows us to deflect projections of others, be our true, authentic selves, and become accountable for our actions, words, and energy. Ascended Master White Matthew encourages us to honor ourselves, the Universe, and other souls we choose to serve by allowing the wisdom that runs through us to be true. You can call upon his energy when needing reminders to be accountable for yourself and as a reminder to be uniquely you.

The animal guide aligned with the pillar of Accountability is the lion. The lion has an aspect of family orientation and being able to be in touch with your inner wisdom and child. At the same time, the lion reminds us to reclaim our might and be accountable for our words and actions. Each member of the pride and the lands they roam over have a role. This is determined by Mother Nature, and each animal interacts and is accountable for the role it plays. The lion will not take more than it needs and encourages us to do what is noble and right with conviction. The lion will guide you to remaining accountable for your actions.

The plant ally allocated to the pillar of Accountability is Frankincense. Frankincense is often used as an oil or resin to anoint those of great wisdom. It is known for being able to open the door between our current place on Earth and the connection with the Universe. Frankincense elevates consciousness and reminds us to be accountable for our actions as it balances out our thoughts, emotions, and patterns whilst taking into account our energy. It allows us to tap into our crown chakra and resonate the frequency needed to allow us to be accountable for ourselves in our practices.

Summary

The pillar of accountability reflects our spiritual purpose of serving souls in the world. When completing this service, you need to be aware of your intentions, your energy, and your purpose when engaging with souls. The crown chakra becomes a conduit for guidance and wisdom from the Universe and needs to be kept in balance to avoid ongoing karmic debts. You can engage the energy of clear quartz to further your intentions and clear your energy field. Remember, be mindful and accountable for your words and actions in all areas of your life.

As we finish our journey with the pillars, we will now move to the additional structures that help link the pillars together. This includes the groundwork of being connected to Earth, the foundation of knowing yourself and others, and the overarching keystone of remembering that we are human. We begin with the groundwork, as this is the underlying structure needed for serving souls and honoring yourself.

CHAPTER 10
GROUNDWORK: BE CONNECTED TO EARTH

The seven pillars of Divine Will, Authenticity, Presence, Willingness to Change, Spiritual Responsibility, Equality, and Accountability form the main part of the Pillars for Life. These are the main areas of spiritual ethics that should guide a soul's practice. However, when creating any structure, we always need to link into the groundwork, foundation, and overall arching keystone that keeps the structure held together. As we continue journeying into Pillars for Life, we have moved to the deepest part of the structure, the groundwork.

In order to build any structure, initial groundwork needs to be created. Whilst many of us think of the foundation as the first thing to be laid, if we do not put in the plans and check the underlying ground, how can we continue to build a sturdy and structurally complete design? Would you build a house on ground that had a large unstable cavern underneath that remained from it being mined for resources? Or would you attempt to build a house without any idea, designs, or plans on how it should look? The answer is no.

Likewise, the groundwork is integral when serving souls. Groundwork is about being connected to Mother Earth. You may prefer the term Gaia, Earth Mother, Pachamama, or something else. Please use whatever resonates for you.

We are electrical beings. This means our energy field carries polarity. Our head is magnetic north, and our feet are magnetic south. Mother Earth is magnetic north. This is why when we stand on the Earth barefoot, our electrical field is rebalanced, and we are grounded in Mother Earth's energy. There have been many studies showing the benefits of grounding, including reduction of inflammation, immune response, wound healing, and assistance in treating chronic inflammatory and autoimmune diseases (Oschman, Chevalier, & Brown, 2015).

Anita Moorjani, a British-born author and speaker known for her near-death experience and subsequent recovery from terminal cancer, stated the connection needed between souls and Mother Earth beautifully: "Going barefoot in nature immediately helps clear your energy. Stepping out onto the sand, putting your feet into the ocean, hugging a tree, all of these clear your energy. Nature is an incredible neutralizer of energy."

As we have learned through the pillars, clearing your energy field and being present are integral for conducting your work with the highest level of integrity. When embarking on any journey to serve others, and this accounts for any field, we need to do the groundwork of our own healing before, during, and after serving clients. This is not meant to be scary, but rather as a gentle reminder to be clear on what you want to share with the world, how you will support yourself and other souls engaging in your service, and ongoing maintenance of your own energy.

Mother Earth has created the perfect tool to achieve all of this. By reconnecting with nature and, in essence, ourselves, we are setting ourselves a solid groundwork in which the other aspects of spiritual ethics can be encompassed. We can then thank Mother Earth and show gratitude by honoring her. If souls only took what they needed rather than indulging in consumerism, the state of the world would be very different.

It is time for us again to walk the land barefoot, plant trees, grow food gardens, nourish the soil, and provide for the animals. To drink from the springs and, in turn, the belly of Mother Earth, to let the wind carry us and the Earth hold us. When we create a practice of balance with Mother Earth, this too will be reflected in our own lives due to our connection with nature. We are nature, and nature is us.

How to Ground

If you are newly embarked on your spiritual journey as a soul, you may have heard the term "grounding" but are not sure what it is. Grounding, sometimes called earthing, is a way for our body to resync its electromagnetic field (EMF) with the Earth. Our bodies have a biofield, or aura, that surrounds us. This means that we are electrical beings and can be impacted by other electrical fields around us.

EMFs are generated by anything that carries a charge. This includes phones, computers, smart watches, TVs, fridges, wi-fi, other humans, and more. These energies do not always mix with our own energy and can lead to us not feeling like us. As we are energy beings, every soul we interact with also interacts with our EMF and can sometimes leave us feeling unbalanced depending on the energy they have.

As a practitioner or a soul who wants to further your own health and well-being, a grounding practice is necessary to assist you in remaining balanced. We have provided some ideas to assist you in grounding with Mother Earth. Use your own discernment to choose a practice that aligns for you. You may even find something more personal based on feedback from your own soul journey.

Practices that may assist you in grounding include:

- Being barefoot: Going outside barefoot is the quickest

and easiest way to ground. Finding a grassy patch with a little bit of dew can make the process even faster. The longer you can stay, the more grounded you will feel, but trust yourself on when you are there long enough. I also love standing on moss or sandstone and feel quite connected with Earth whilst doing this.

- Meditation: A grounding meditation is another way you can connect with the Earth if you aren't able to go barefoot. Here is a simple version of this meditation:

  - Start by closing your eyes and just breathing in through your nose and out through your mouth (if you can).
  - Feel your sit bones in the chair and your feet on the Earth.
  - Imagine your feet are sinking into the floor beneath you, pushing further down.
  - Feel or imagine vines or cords connecting you deep into the heart of Mother Earth, making you feel earthed and grounded.
  - Slowly open your eyes when you are ready and wiggle your fingers and toes.

- Crystals: You can use different crystals to make you feel more grounded and connected with the Earth. This is due to the crystals' energy. Crystals include (but are not limited to) tiger's eye, smoky quartz, jasper, hematite, obsidian, black tourmaline, unakite, agate, amber, aragonite, green opal, hawk's eye, lava stone, mookaite, onyx, and petrified wood.

- Rock/sea salt: Placing a piece of rock salt (Celtic or a good quality sea salt) under your tongue can help you feel grounded as the natural frequency of rock salt is to the Earth.

- Root vegetables: Eating root vegetables (e.g., carrots, sweet potatoes, or anything that grows in the ground) can also help you feel grounded. As they come from the Earth, they help our energy rebalance to the Earth as we consume them.

- Herbs/oils: If the herb is from a root or calming flower, it can help us feel connected to the ground. Herbs for grounding include chamomile, lavender, valerian root, passionflower, ashwagandha, lemon balm, and holy basil. There are also essential oils that contain properties to assist with your grounding by adjusting the frequency of your body. These include but are not limited to vetiver, sandalwood, cedarwood, frankincense, and myrrh.

Earth Chakra

The earth chakra is located just under the soles of our feet and assists with connecting to Mother Earth. It is linked to the Earth Star in the auric field and helps us to anchor into the Earth. As we are human, we are also connected to nature. Animals are easily able to remember their connection with nature and, in turn, tune their earth chakra to Mother Earth.

We have been disconnected through the loss of ceremony, the pavement of land, and the amnesia of remembering how to honor Mother Earth and respect what she gives us. Focusing on reconnecting with this chakra strengthens our relationships with Mother Earth and the groundwork upon which we need to build ourselves. Spending time barefoot in nature is needed for grounding, healing, and reminding our bodies of the amazing connection we have with Mother Earth and the gifts she has bestowed upon us in order to live.

The trees work in synergy with us to clean our air and provide us with more oxygen. The land grows food for us to eat, which we can use to nourish our bodies. The water flows and purifies itself using the rocks and sand to provide us with water to hydrate our bodies. The sun provides us with rays of light to restore our Vitamin D and, in turn, allow chemical processes to occur in our body that protect our immune system. We are one with nature, and nature is one with us. Tuning our Earth Star and allowing ourselves to connect more will foster our ability to expand whilst keeping ourselves anchored to Mother Earth.

Crystal Connection

The crystal that has been assigned to the groundwork is red jasper. As stated earlier, you may have a different crystal that resonates for you in relation to being connected to Mother Earth and the Earth Star chakra. Please trust your intuition and use what aligns for you.

Please keep in mind that all crystals will connect you to Mother Earth. Due to the plane of existence in which crystals are created, they are gifts and blessings from the energy of the Universe that can be used to assist with healing and clearing energy. In turn, Mother Earth continues to gift us crystals in rocks washed up on the beach, in hidden caves across the world, and even as natural disasters create the landscape for new crystals to be created.

In particular, red jasper reminds us that we are not alone in this great, big Universe. Rather, we are connected, particularly through Mother Earth, and we are grounded into our natural state. Just as Mother Earth brings us with a nurturing energy, so too does red jasper. It allows you to put ideas into action whilst also giving you honesty, strength, and courage in difficult situations.

Guide or Guardian Connection

As mentioned, the guides and guardians described in relation to the groundwork are based on energies that have been channeled through. If you have other guides or guardians who align more with the energies of the groundwork, trust your intuition and discernment to evoke these energies. Alternatively, if you feel pulled to research the guides or guardians suggested, then allow that to happen.

The guardian who oversees the groundwork is Mother Earth. Mother Earth goes by many names, including Gaia, Pachamama, Earth Goddess, and many others. She reminds us that we are nature, we come from nature, and we are one with nature. By honoring and calling upon Mother Earth, we are, in turn, honoring ourselves and any soul we work with. What better way to be reminded that we are connected than by calling on Mother Earth and allowing her energy to flow through us?

The animal guide aligned with the groundwork is the turtle. The turtle reminds us to stay true to our path and the need to choose to reconnect with Mother Earth. He is able to transmute the energy of feeling out of balance or disconnected from ourselves, to come back to the center and ground back in with nature. Additionally, the turtle helps your transformation into a fully actualized spiritual being living on Mother Earth by alchemizing your soul energy with Mother Nature.

The plant ally allocated to the groundwork is the flannel flower. The flannel flower symbolizes purity, rebirth, and fresh starts, as well as the ability for us to be spiritually connected to the land. This connection with Mother Earth is needed for the beauty and medicine of Flannel Flower to be shared with the world. The flannel flower is here to remind us of the cycles of life and the need to maintain a deep connection with the nature in which we are part.

Summary

In order to have any structure, we need an established and strong groundwork beneath us on which we can build a foundation. The groundwork that we are connected to every day is Mother Earth. By honoring and respecting our relationships with our world and anchoring our Earth Star, we are able to create a means to amplify our spiritual development and connect with other souls who allow us to serve them. We are nature, and nature is us. Having a daily practice of grounding and connecting to Mother Earth will assist in all aspects of your body, mind, and soul.

As we have learned the importance of groundwork which underlies the Pillars for Life, with our connection to nature, it is time to venture to the foundation, the very footings on which the Pillars for Life are built. We journey into knowing yourself and others to see how this underpins the Pillars for Life.

CHAPTER 11
FOUNDATION: KNOWING YOURSELF AND OTHERS

The foundation of any structure needs to be solid and secure. This is no different when engaging in spiritual ethics and incorporating the Pillars for Life into your life. However, in this case, the foundation is you. As you are the conduit for the Universe, you need to have a clear awareness of yourself and the souls who choose to work with you. This includes being aware of when your body needs to rest or when you need an active recovery to allow you to continue to serve.

It has been emphasized several times throughout the pillars that you need to be responsible for your own spiritual hygiene. This, too, goes for ensuring your body is receiving the nutrients and care it needs to continue to support you in serving others. Looking after just your mind and spirit will not serve you for long. It is necessary to ensure the body aspect is also addressed.

Our body is the vehicle that we have chosen to serve our soul at this time. When it is neglected, our ability to tune in with our mind and spirit becomes more difficult, as does our ability to serve others. Neglecting our body and its signs for attunement is similar to neglecting the fuel/gas light on your car dashboard and then wondering why the car stops working. We are often quick to serve and assist others but neglect to care for our own bodies and health.

When you feel like resting, it is important that you honor this and do so. You will find if you continue to ignore the signs to rest, the Universe will give you a reminder or create a situation that will result in you needing to do so. I've personally had this happen to me several times over my life, usually when I was refusing to rest and slow down.

The biggest example was during the pandemic and COVID-19 restrictions. I was looking after my health and my body whilst continuing to run my company and navigating the various gauntlets placed on us by the ever-changing government regulations. I was incredibly healthy and well, but my adrenals needed to slow down. I kept pushing, and fortunately, instead of burning myself out, the Universe created a situation that saw me restricted to my home for three weeks, and I was unable to leave. This made me need to work from home, reduce my client load, and give myself some much-needed recovery. If I am honest—I was so grateful. I loved that time I got to be at home and rest. However, should I not have received that divine intervention, I feel my body would have stopped working for me how I needed it to in order to survive that time.

This is similar to serving souls. If you feel that your energy is not aligned and you are uncomfortable providing others with the care they need, be open to this. Continuing to serve this soul can impact both your body (physically and energetically) and health. When you serve from a place of uncertainty, it opens your energy field to being imprinted by others' energy, which, in turn, can impact your body physically. It is times like this that you need to be vulnerable and authentic, connect with yourself, and find the courage to have a conversation with the soul you are serving.

For example, a soul comes to you as a body worker, asking for assistance with some back pain. As you begin to work on the body, you feel there is a deep emotional connection to this back pain that you cannot shift. It is in this moment that you need to discern if the soul would be open to further assistance from another practitioner, as this is not an area you are comfortable addressing because you do not have the skill set to do so. Knowing yourself and others, including other souls to refer to, is important in the moment to ensure the care of the soul is for the highest and greatest good. In this case, that means supporting them in finding the right connection to further them on their soul journey.

Similarly, if you are seeking a service from someone to address your own physical, emotional, or spiritual well-being, knowing yourself is important. You want to be aware of how you feel before a session, what your energy is versus someone else's, and that you are able to express what you need. If you feel you did not achieve the desired experience or left feeling different in a negative way, this is feedback from your soul letting you know that this may not be the practitioner for you. Again, remember it is ok to ask questions of yourself and the practitioner. Be open and curious as to what comes through.

The Shadow

Shadow work is not something to be feared but to be embraced. We all have shadows—these are our fears, our flaws, our wounds. The aspects of our beliefs and traumas that have shaped us into fearing our own potential. As you move through your spiritual journey and grow as a soul, shadow work is an integral part of getting to know yourself so you are no longer limited by your own fears and beliefs.

The greatest form of love comes from loving the parts of you that are deemed "unlovable." Sending love to those who wronged you, those who created trauma, and the aspects of yourself that you do not like allows you to accept yourself as whole and know that we are not meant to be perfect. The challenge and growth of a soul come from realizing and accepting that we are imperfect, that we are enough, and that it is our journey. By accepting and loving the shadow part of ourselves, you realize you are whole and do not need to be fixed. Rather, you are choosing to change yourself, just as those who choose you as a practitioner are whole and seek your assistance to serve them to change an aspect of themselves. This may be shifting pain or choosing to enter a new part of their spiritual journey. Either way, they are seeking your assistance to change an aspect of themselves that needs to be accepted and loved.

When beginning my shadow work, I was led to a soul fragment (this may be a past life, parallel life, or whatever concept resonates for you) where there was much darkness. This aspect of me was abused by her partner and made to feel weak, inadequate, and like she needed to be beaten into submission. One evening of the regular abuse, she whispered to her partner, "I am going to kill you one day," to which he laughed. A week later, she did exactly this with some broken glass and not a hint of remorse as she watched him die in front of her. She then traveled around the country, listening for stories or hints of abuse and ending the man's life who caused it. Initially, I found it shocking that life could be so expendable, as well as the lack of love this version of myself experienced.

However, when speaking to this version of myself, I realized what I was missing. Love. I had never been told or shown love. When I looked myself in the eye and said, "I am sorry, please forgive me, thank you, and I love you," this version of myself broke down in tears and cried, never having ever heard those words. I loved this version of myself, even though it was dark and empty. I integrated the shadow aspect of my soul karma and allowed it to make me whole.

Whilst this is an extreme example, that part of me needed love just as much as the aspects I do like about myself. It is through loving the unlovable and accepting that we are exactly how we are meant to be that we are able to work with our shadows and embrace all aspects of ourselves. Allow yourself time to integrate what comes through, be gracious with yourself, and know the shadows do not define who you are. The shadows are what you overcome and integrate to become an amazing soul full of unconditional love for yourself.

Rescheduling

We, as those souls who choose to serve others, often find it difficult to cancel a day of appointments when we are not feeling ourselves. However, if you are out of alignment and not aware of what your energy is doing, this can be detrimental both to yourself and the souls you are serving that day. Whilst you may feel financial strain or time constraints make it difficult to cancel, if you are not able to be fully present and spiritually responsible, especially for your energy, the session is going to result in further detriment to all those involved and, in turn, is not reflective of the highest and greatest good.

Therefore, it is ok to reschedule. It is ok to look after yourself in regard to your body, mind, and soul, especially when you feel your energy is not in alignment. Give yourself permission to rest and give yourself the grace and courage to be vulnerable and speak up when you need to reschedule a session. You are human, and so are the souls who choose to work with you. It is important to honor this.

These are some guiding questions to help you feel into what the reason for needing to cancel and reschedule. This can be used to assist in reflecting upon your current energy and provide next steps as well:

- Have you checked the reason you feel like canceling?
- Have you been checking your spiritual hygiene and energy? Clearing out anything that does not belong.
- Have you tried to reset your energy through practices such as grounding and field clearing?
- Are you able to show up and serve the best way you can

despite feeling to cancel?
- How can you ensure that your soul's energy is restored so you are able to return to serving?
- Have you ensured that options are provided and that you follow up with the reschedule when you are able to?

Soul Star Chakra

The soul star chakra is needed to balance our other chakras. It links into our higher self (the true expression of our soul) as well as the light of the Universe. It allows you to navigate the Akashic Records (a record of everything that has, is, and will be on your current time frame) and gives you a deeper understanding of your karma. This is essential for knowing oneself as well as beginning to understand the relationship you have with others. This energy center is responsible for recharging your soul with its purpose whilst also keeping you balanced.

In our auric layer, this chakra is linked to your Real Self. This is the layer that holds information around our soul contracts with others we choose to serve, have relationships with, or who come into our lives. It underpins the need to know yourself and others and to be aware that some people come into our lives for a season and do not need to stay longer.

Crystal Connection

The crystal that has been assigned to the foundation of knowing yourself and others is selenite. As stated earlier, you may have a different crystal that resonates for you in relation to knowing yourself and others and the soul star chakra. Please trust your intuition and use what aligns for you.

Selenite is known as an angelic stone that can purify energies—including those of other stones. It can absorb negative energy and transmute this for the highest and greatest good. Selenite needs to be cleared in the sunlight or moonlight due to its absorbent nature, which also means it is impacted in water. Selenite helps you connect with the spiritual realm and, in turn, anchors you in your auric field and the vibration of Earth. This crystal emanates itself as the foundation of connecting ourselves to all aspects and planes of existence.

Guide or Guardian Connection

As mentioned, the guides and guardians described in relation to the foundation are based on energies that have been channeled through. If you have other guides or guardians who align more with the energies of the foundation, trust your intuition and discernment to evoke these energies. Alternatively, if you feel pulled to research the guides or guardians suggested, then allow that to happen, too.

The guardian who oversees the foundation is Goddess Isis. Isis helps us remember our true selves whilst creating the capacity to be intimate and connect with our divine feminine. Isis is there to allow you to lead from your heart and be creative in your chosen practice whilst mastering the magic this world has to offer. By embracing her shadow and light, Isis was able to encompass the energy of knowing herself and others and used this to guide those whom she led. She was able to create the foundation of the life she wanted and build this in alignment with her soul.

The animal guide aligned with the foundation is the beaver spirit. The beaver spirit reminds us that we are connected to the Universe and that by laying a solid foundation, we can create the lives we want. Be clear on what you value and your standards; then, in turn, you will be able to serve yourself and others to create a life aligned to your purpose.

The plant ally allocated to the foundation is mugwort. Mugwort is known for her properties with eliciting lucid dreaming. However, her ability to allow us to ground and organize our thoughts is not discussed as much. When wanting to know ourselves and others, mugwort can allow for exploration through our dreams whilst also balancing out our bodies and cleansing what is no longer needed. You can call in mugwort and her strength to help you stand true in your standards and values whilst also supporting others.

Summary

In order to have any structure, we need a strong foundation, which, in this case, is our body and health. In the case of the Pillars for Life and spiritual ethics, this involves you being accountable for knowing yourself and others. It is about taking responsibility for your energy, connecting to an intent for the highest and greatest good whilst also tuning into Earth's vibration. Without knowing yourself, you are unable to support others in a way that creates synergy. In turn, the foundation is linked to your soul star chakra and real self-auric layer to act as a reminder that you are energy, and this energy needs to be strong and clear when you are working with the energy of another.

As we have established the underlying supports for the Pillars for Life, we now move on to the Keystone—the main aspect that brings the structure together. This is the final aspect of Pillars for Life and spiritual ethics. It is through the Keystone and remembering that we are human that we are then able to integrate the groundwork, foundation, and Pillars for Life into our practice and allow us to serve other souls for the highest and greatest good.

CHAPTER 12
KEYSTONE: REMEMBER TO BE HUMAN

A keystone in a structure is the central stone that locks everything together. This is the precipice behind this key piece of the Pillars for Life and spiritual ethics. You have chosen to incarnate as a human in this lifetime. In turn, this is why we experience emotions and have an urge in our hearts to connect to something greater. It is through our connection with the Universe that our humanity can be seen as a gift. The keystone is the penultimate part of the Pillars for Life, as without being human, all the other components of the Spiritual Ethics Framework would not exist. It brings and holds together each of the pillars as well as securing them to the groundwork and foundation.

If we do not go through a human experience, we would not be able to experience the wonder that the Universe has created. We are here on planet Earth, having a human experience. This is for a reason, as this is what your soul has chosen to do. Embrace it. Allow emotions to happen, but let others know it is ok to be human. When we own our emotions and let them be free, which is truly part of the human experience, then we can connect with each other through the heart and, in turn, uplift those around us.

We are all mirrors of each other. Each soul incarnated on Earth contains the same essence of the spark of creation as the Universe, which, in turn, makes us all connected. Our unique DNA of 23 pairs was not by accident but by evolutionary design to enable us to connect fully with the Universe and find our way through our human experience back to the Universe and the start of our being.

Staying Connected

We are each created as a blessing on this Earth in our unique expression of our DNA code and, in turn, our uniquely human expression. Whilst you may meet other souls who encompass similar traits, you will never be exactly the same due to the emotional and life events that impact your spiritual epigenetics. This leads to a unique expression of your traits and human design and, in turn, makes each of us unique.

As a soul unpacks their beliefs, values, trauma, emotions, and other aspects of their spiritual epigenetics, they will feel pulled to return to their connection with the Universe. This will sometimes be done easily, and other times, it may require diligent practice in order to stay connected to the Universe and your spiritual team.

It does not matter what practice you choose to invoke this connection. However, what matters is the intention to do this on a daily basis and also encompass the other aspects of Spiritual Ethics.

Meditation, connecting with nature, prayer, mindful movement, free writing, somatic experiences, and breathwork are just a few examples of connecting with the Universe. These connections strengthen with each intentional moment, and this is where the spiritual work is done. Connecting with the Universe allows you to embody your light and, in turn, bring the highest and greatest good into everything you do.

It is your responsibility to commit to this daily practice in whichever way resonates for you. Remember, we are all unique, and we all have a unique process of connecting to the Universe.

This may not resonate for some souls. Trust what aligns for you and honor the unique process you create.

For example, I ventured into the realm of breathwork after being guided by a mentor. I went in with an open mind, and as I heard other souls recall what had taken place for them, I knew and felt my experience was not going to be the pleasant, joyful one that others had described. As I entered into the magic of breathwork, I went through an initiation of reclaiming my power at the time of death in other incarnations, underwent psychic surgery in which I felt all the pain, and faced shadows that needed to be shifted. As we all reflected at the end, some souls had shadow experiences whilst others had blissful moments they were eager to return to. This experience led to a chain of events that needed to occur for me to reclaim my power and shift to my next level of spiritual development.

It took me nearly a year before I was ready to return to this practice. My soul needed that time to integrate, and whilst others attended each month or more regularly, this was not for me at the time. My following breathwork experiences were far less traumatic than my original experience and left me in those blissful and expansive states. However, I needed to go through the shadow work in order to grow into the soul that would be able to receive the gifts I continually evolve.

Breathwork is not a daily practice for me, whilst for other souls, it may be. However, I am aware of how to use it more regularly and also trust my intuition when it is pulled to do a deeper, guided session. My daily practice evolved from these events and now allows me to connect directly with the Universe each day in a manner unique to me and by asking how I can serve.

Being open and curious and following what feels aligned for you will allow you to create a spiritual connection unique to you and allow you to tap into an infinite source of wisdom. Create a daily practice that feels aligned and keep your connection strong and open. A daily practice also allows you to become more connected with yourself, including your body, mind, and soul, so that you can be led to the right practitioners.

As souls choosing to serve others, it is important to be aware that we all have a spiritual connection. The strength of this connection truly comes down to your commitment and choice to be led by the Universe into the next aspect of your life.

Divine Chakra

The divine chakra (also called the Divine Gateway) is the highest frequency energetic center connected to our human existence. It has a unique relationship with each chakra and a particularly strong connection with our heart chakra. The divine chakra is our direct connection to the Universe and is essential for us to remain connected to the Universe. It is our pathway back to home, and it also allows us to remain human and have a human experience. It is a permanent link between the Universe and us as the creation.

This chakra is linked to the Divine Gateway in our auric field. This is a unique connection as it pulls in energy from the portal created by our hearts. In essence, the energy in the divine gateway level of the auric field links with your internal heart energy and connects our human and divine selves. It forms a vortex with the energy field (energy egg) radiating from our heart. In addition, the Divine Gateway is able to balance and redistribute energy across other auric layers, as well as chakras, to maintain life by giving energy so that we can continue to live as humans.

Crystal Connection

The crystal that has been assigned to the keystone of Remembering to be Human is celestite. As stated earlier, you may have a different crystal that resonates for you in remembering to be human and the divine chakra. Please trust your intuition and use what aligns for you.

Celestite is a crystal known for allowing a connection with the higher realms and the Universe. It inspires divine energies whilst also uplifting moods and energy to shift anxiety and heaviness. Celestite can also help magnify your clairs (soul gifts), particularly clairvoyancy (clear seeing), and calls in your spirit team and the Universe to support you. In addition, it can further your spiritual development and, in turn, nurture your connection as a human to the Universe.

Guide or Guardian Connection

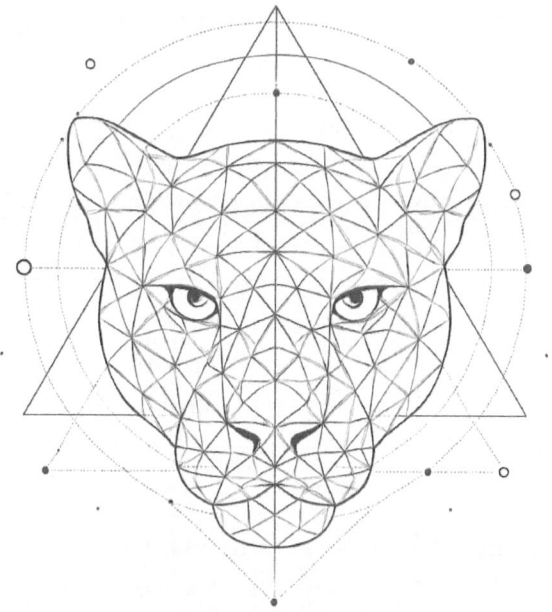

As mentioned, the guides and guardians described in relation to the keystone are based on energies that have been channeled through. If you have other guides or guardians who align more with the energies of the keystone, trust your intuition and discernment to evoke these energies. Alternatively, if you feel pulled to research the guides or guardians suggested, then allow that to happen.

The guardian who oversees the keystone is Mother Mary. Mother Mary reminds us to love unconditionally—to feel connected, to lead from our hearts, and to heal our relationships with others in order to move forward in our lives. She encourages us to create abundance and follow our bliss whilst letting go of our limiting beliefs and that we are infinite. Despite being human, we still have the capability to connect with the energy of the Universe and create an infinite potential to let go of our old identities and move into one that connects us on all levels. Mother Mary allows us to maximize our human experience whilst living a life of our highest potential.

The animal guide aligned with the keystone is the jaguar. The jaguar is called upon to improve psychic awareness. She is powerful and brings medicine when needed, as well as a level of protection. The jaguar can be used as a bridge between Earth and the Universe as you tap into higher realms and the Universe. She awakens your soul to its true purpose and power whilst allowing you to embrace your shadows and connect with all aspects of yourself in your human experience. The jaguar will support you when you need strength and courage and bring back the magic you are missing from your life.

The plant ally allocated to the keystone is cedarwood. Cedarwood stands tall in its strength whilst anchoring in the ground. It reminds us to be confident and instills a sense of confidence. It is not always an easy ride, and despite the highs and lows of life, cedarwood brings in his energy of security when we are unsure of who we are. He allows us to cope with the stresses and strains of life and, in turn, come back to who we are in our human form. Additionally, cedarwood helps provide us with emotional security and returns us to a grounded state where we can tune in with our hearts and truly honor what it means to be human.

Summary

In order to complete a structure, such as a bridge, a keystone is needed. This is the energy behind the keystone of "Remember to Be Human." We chose to incarnate on Earth to have a human experience. It is through this experience that we are also able to create a connection with the Universe for guidance and to remind us of our infinite wisdom and capability of who we are. By allowing our Divine Gateway to remain clear and open, we are able to have a permanent link with the Universe, which supports our connection when serving other souls.

CHAPTER 13 BRINGING IT ALL TOGETHER

Spiritual Ethics are guidelines for how to serve when engaging other souls in your chosen modality. They also underpin a way to conduct yourself in your everyday life. Being human means that we are not always perfect; however, it does not prevent us from making a conscious effort to embody these guidelines into our everyday practice and how we conduct ourselves. Spiritual Ethics is a way of life that can be transmuted through every aspect of our lives.

Pillar of Spiritual Ethics	Crystal	Guardian	Animal Guide	Plant Ally
Keystone	Celestite	Mother Mary	Jaguar	Cedarwood
Foundation	Selenite	Goddess Isis	Beaver	Mugwort
Ground work	Red Jasper	Mother Earth/Gaia	Turtle	Flannel Flower
Accountability	Clear Quartz	Ascended Master White Matthew	Lion	Frankincense
Equality	Amethyst	Saint Germain	Emu	Lotus
Spiritual Responsibility	Aquamarine	Achangel Bath Kol	Dolphin	Pine
Willingness to Change	Rose Quartz	Jesua/ Yeshua	Butterfly	Rose
Presence	Citrine	God Ra	Eagle	Sunflower
Authenticity	Amber	Goddess Freya	Wolf	Sandalwood
Divine Will	Obsidian	Goddess Kali	Elephant	Eucalypts

The design of the pillars, groundwork, foundation, and keystone aim to reflect the complex tapestry of interwoven ideals and aspects that arise in serving other souls. Whilst it may not address all elements of your chosen practice, it is aimed to help you evolve your practice for the highest good of all souls involved. Again, use your own discernment when serving a soul under these principles and choose what aligns with you. The table below summarizes the connection between the pillars, groundwork, foundation, and keystone with the corresponding crystals, guides, and allies.

Any exchange with another soul involves energy. As such, it is important to keep your energy centers and field balanced and aligned so that you are able to express your true self. Additionally, this governs the principles behind choosing crystals and guides or guardians for each aspect. Be connected with your intuition and trust what aligns for you.

As you move forward in your service to others, remember to uphold the same values in your everyday life. Being and acting in two different energy systems based on who you are with or who you are serving is not reflective of a soul embodying its true self and showing up authentically. Nor does it reflect one's Spiritual Responsibility, accountability, or knowing yourself and others. It is time to be authentically you and vulnerable in every aspect of your life. If you are unsure how this would be represented, reconnect with your heart energy and receive the wisdom from there. Connect with the Universe and ask for guidance. Follow your joy and passion, and trust that where you feel most aligned is where your true self resides.

It is true we are always evolving as we continue on our journey as humans. This means that other souls will come and go into our lives as our frequency, vibration, and true self continue to evolve. We give gratitude in those moments, even if we cannot always see the good, and trust the flow and the plan that the Universe has for us.

You are not designed to be alone, especially if you are a soul who has chosen to serve others. At times, we may feel lonely and misunderstood. These are the moments when it is important to come back to your heart, connect with your intuition and the Universe, and allow wisdom to come through. Do not put conditions on yourself or limit the infinite potential that is within you. Trust that the Universe has a plan. As you continue to move through the lessons that life bestows upon you, an attitude of gratitude is going to allow you more grace and ease than being resistant and falling into a victim mindset.

Trust that Spiritual Ethics is a compass in these moments. That you come back to you and your divine self and allow the wisdom and guidance to come through. Surround yourself with souls who also choose to serve and want to elevate the human experience whilst encompassing the energy of Spiritual Ethics. Our lives are always a choice. There is no wrong choice, just one that will move you further on your journey or allow you to remain on the same path. Your Divine Will is a true gift and one to always recall.

Thank you for choosing to journey through Spiritual Ethics and being open to the guidance and lessons shared by the Universe. As you continue on your path of serving souls, it is my hope that these guidelines allow you to feel more aligned with yourself, those you serve, and the practice you have chosen to share with the world. May you always shine your light brightly and be committed to the highest and greatest timeline for yourself and all souls who choose to embrace and spread your light.

REFERENCES

Articles

Oschman JL, Chevalier G, Brown R. The effects of grounding (earthing) on inflammation, the immune response, wound healing, and prevention and treatment of chronic inflammatory and autoimmune diseases. J Inflamm Res. 2015 Mar 24;8:83-96. doi: 10.2147/JIR.S69656. PMID: 25848315; PMCID: PMC4378297.

Books

Collete Baron-Reid: The Spirit Animal Oracle Guidebook

Judith Collins 'How to See and Read the Human Aura: A Practical Guide'

Cyndi Dale 'The Subtle Body: An Encyclopedia of Your Energetic Anatomy'

Susan Gregg 'Angels, Spirit Guides and Goddesses: A guide to working with 100 divine beings in your daily life'.

Susan Gregg 'The Complete Encyclopedia of Angels: A Guide to 200 Celestial Beings to Help, Heal and Assist You in Everyday Life'.

Spirit Magicka Crystals 'Crystal Compendium'

Michael Talbot 'The Holographic Universe'

Cassie Uhl 'The Zenned Out Guide to Understanding Auras: Your Handbook to Seeing, Reading, and Protecting Your Aura'.

Websites

https://www.cassieuhl.com/blog/what-is-the-soul-star-chakra-and-how-to-connect-to-it

https://stellarcrystalcompany.com/collections/earth-star

Snug Scent: https://snugscent.co.uk/snug-scent-blog/about-smudging/what-are-smudge-sticks-and-what-do-they-do/

https://whatismyspiritanimal.com/

https://salvatorebattaglia.com.au/blogs/mongraphs

https://archangeloracle.com/2017/01/25/ascended-master-white-matthew-and-danburite/

https://bloomcollege.com.au/blog/flannel-flower-natures-delicate-beauty/

https://www.herbalreality.com/herb/mugwort/#traditional-energetic-actions

ACKNOWLEDGEMENT

With heartfelt gratitude, I acknowledge the talented individuals who helped bring *Pillars for Life* into being.

To **Carli Sheriff** for being my guide, my mentor, and for being the initial channel for this book. I am blessed for your guidance and support.

The book cover and design were beautifully crafted by my amazing husband, **Peter Jones**, whose creative vision captured the essence of this work with clarity and elegance. Thank you for putting up with my continuous debate over fonts.

The illustrations for *Pillars for Life* were lovingly created by **Teck Nyiap**, whose artistry gave form to the spiritual teachings and brought the Pillars to life in a powerful visual way that was beyond my imagination.

Deep thanks to **Lia Ottaviano** for her thoughtful editing and care in shaping the written word, ensuring the message remained clear, grounded, and aligned.

To **Jane Barlow Christensen** for writing and sharing such beautiful words and capturing the essence of the book.

To each of you — thank you for your part in this co-creation.

ABOUT THE AUTHOR

Catherine Crestani

Catherine Crestani is a leadership coach, intuitive healer, podcaster, author and international speaker who shares messages of empowerment through many modalities. With nearly two decades of experience working in allied health and running successful 6-figure companies, Catherine chose to step out of her roles to focus on her health, her family and most importantly her connection to herself through listening to her intuition.

Catherine's spiritual journey began in 2021, as she searched for fulfillment outside the lifestyle she had built, based on other's expectations. As she underwent a rapid awakening, Catherine was gifted the outline for Pillars for Life on a quest to ensure that the souls who enlisted her services were receiving messages and healing for their highest and greatest good. She continued to evolve her gifts and serves her clients through using her knowledge, leadership skills, inner wisdom, energy medicine, real life examples, and compassion to achieve results.

Catherine currently resides in Australia and her primary focus is being a mom to her son and building a life with her husband that reflects their version of success. She enjoys learning and connecting with souls across the world through her podcast,

Willow Healing Matters, and loves exploring nature in her free time.

www.ingramcontent.com/pod-product-compliance
Lightning Source LLC
Chambersburg PA
CBHW060402080526
44583CB00012B/438